ALL ABOUT Blue Budgerigars

by

Roy Stringer
and
Fred Wright

First Published 1993

ISBN 0 9518145 3 2

Typeset in New Century Schoolbook and Printed in Britain by Spottiswoode Ballantyne, Colchester, Essex, England. Published by Roy Stringer Publications, Somerdale Cottage, Station Road, Westbury, Shropshire.

CONTENTS

Acknowledgements

Roy Stringer and Fred Wright gratefully acknowledge the kindness of Eric Peake in offering us the idea for this series of books and for painting the lovely Skyblue Budgerigar on the cover, the great effort put in by Les Lockey, himself a very successful champion breeder, exhibitor and judge of Budgerigars, in travelling around Britain to take photographs of the experts, their birdrooms and – most importantly – their superb Blue Budgerigars specifically for this book, Harry Bryan, for delving into his wonderful memory to recall some outstanding Blues from the past, Brian Byles, Editor of *Cage & Aviary Birds* and Peter Moss, Editor of *Bird keeper* for their support and advice during the book's preparation. Then, of course, there are the experts who have answered dozens of questions in our quest to discover what it is that has brought them success at the highest levels with Blue Budgerigars; Derrick Bowley, Brian Byles, Gren and Pat Norris and Joe Sabella. We thank them all.

FOREWORD

by Eric Peake

When, in 1992, the first two books in this series were published one of my ambitions was fulfilled. For years I had contemplated writing such a series, dealing with different varieties and featuring the views of top breeders. It became obvious that my painting commitments were pushing this prospect further into the future so I passed the idea to Roy Stringer and Fred Wright.

My belief that they would do the idea justice was amply justified by the excellence and popularity of *All About Greens* and *All About Red-eyes.* I was delighted to be asked to paint the covers for the books and to contribute the forewords, based on what I have observed when painting both the "Ideals" for several national societies and specific Budgerigars that have won major prizes. This, the fourth book, deals with the Blues, made up of the Skyblue, Cobalt, Mauve and the striking Violet.

The Skyblue, the lightest of the three shades, is the most numerous of the group. Even so, depth of colour is all important, though difficult to achieve. Casting my mind back I can recall only a few that have stood out in this respect. It is also difficult to maintain the depth of black in the markings and the use of Opalines has not helped by creating a blue cast around the wing butts and neck. With the notable exceptions of some outstanding specimens, Skyblues tend to lack in size and head quality - possibly a function of the Blue factor. One of the most beautiful Skyblues I have ever seen was Derrick Bowley's hen which took the best opposite sex award at the Budgerigar Society Club Show. Another that deserves a mention is Norris & Baldry's (later to be Mr & Mrs Norris) Skyblue cock that went one better and took the best in show award at the same event.

Cobalts are Blues of the medium shade and are even more difficult to breed to the highest standards. The achievement of the novice Richmond partnership in taking the best in show trophy at the BS Club Show in 1992 with a Cobalt cock was a significant step forward in the story of this variety.

Mauves, being the dark members of the Blue series, have been neglected for many years and a good exhibition specimen is now a rarity. Although they have their own characteristic beauty, Mauves cannot compete with their lighter counterparts.

Although the Violet factor can be combined with any colour, it is when it combines with Cobalt to give us the visual Violet that we get the most vivid coloration ever seen in Budgerigars. Sometimes the illusion is created that the edges of their body feathers are tinged with pink. I recall with pleasure the Violets of the Danecourt stud, Harry Bryan and William Watmough (I was honoured to paint a Violet on the cover of a later edition of his book, *The Cult of the Budgerigar*). Although it is difficult to breed Violets in large quantities, anyone attempting to do so will be adding to the beauty of Budgerigars.

INTRODUCING THE BLUES

Next time you gaze into an aviary of Budgerigars and see the wonderful array of colours, just cast your mind back 100 years to the end of the 19th century. If you had looked into a Budgerigar aviary then, you would have been seeing Green upon Green upon Green. This is not surprising because the story of the domesticated Budgerigar began only in 1840 when explorer, John Gould, brought the first pair of Budgerigars to England, from the Liverpool Plain of Southern Australia. Like every other wild Budgerigar, they were Green. After 30 years of breeding Budgerigars in captivity the first colour mutation, the Light Yellow, was established.

The second mutation, Blue, was first reported in Belgium in 1878, but this line disappeared without trace. Just three years later, in 1881, another Blue appeared and this line was established. Mr Van de Snickt wrote of the first Blues: "No bird in the world has caused so much admiration and, at the same time, so many expectations." He was promised two Blue hens but when he went to collect them they were found dead on their eggs. Forty years later they were still few and far between.

Those Blues that did appear in those early days tended to be weakly specimens. Stories abounded of their colour fading until they were almost white. Theories sprang up that the further a Budgerigar's colour varied from the wild-type Green, the weaker it would be. Present experience of Blue Budgerigars does not support these reports.

The first Blue Budgerigars to arrived in the UK in 1910 and came from the aviaries of Mr Pauvvels in Belgium. His aviary manager, Mr O. Millsum (a noted exhibitor of rabbits) claimed that these came from a family of Dutch origin which had been maintained since 1885. A Blue was displayed at a Zoological Society meeting late in 1910. Others were exhibited at London's Horticultural Hall shortly afterwards and at Crystal Palace in 1911. Blues were first bred in Britain in 1912 and the selling price at that time was around £14 a pair. All of these Blues were what we now call Skyblues, because the Dark factor which created Cobalts and Mauves had not been established at that time. By 1918, a "coals to Newcastle" situation had developed and Budgerigars were being sent to Australia – because they were Skyblues – though the early imports were not very successful.

Aviculturist, George Hedges, played a large part in the developments that followed. While he was in charge of Mme Lescallier's collection in France, he produced the first Cobalt Budgerigar. He became Mrs Dalton Burgess's aviary attendant and the first Mauves appeared in her collection (and Mme Lescallier's) in 1924. Until their present names became generally accepted, terms such as Royal Blue and Iris were used to describe the Cobalt. Mauves were variously known as French Greys, Lilacs and Lavenders.

It was in the mid-1920s that the Budgerigar world went mad. Because Blue Budgerigars became fashionable in Japan, the price of a pair of Skyblues leapt up from £10 to more than £100. Cobalts and Mauves could command £150 a pair. In 1927 prices rose even higher, to £125 a pair for Skyblues and £175 for Cobalts and Mauves. Fortunes were made, but the bubble burst and the boom ended even more quickly than it had begun.

Even at that frenzied time, the beauty of Blue Budgerigars meant more to some breeders than their monetary value. An early enthusiast, Mr Pracht, expressed this sentiment in 1924 with the following words: "The long cherished hope is fulfilled. Before me is an observation cage with the precious contents – a couple of absolutely Blue Budgerigars. Everybody who sees them is as enchanted as I am." However, he feared that when they became more numerous they would no longer be appreciated. "Whatever appears in large quantities, though ever so pretty, soon suffers neglect." Fortunately generations of Blue Budgerigar breeders have proved him wrong. Pretty they are, but certainly not neglected.

Another, quite brilliant, dimension was added to the already glittering range of Blue Budgerigars, in the 1930s, when the Violet mutation was established. They may have existed before and been identified as richly-coloured Cobalts, but it was soon established that they were a variety apart. According to the late Cyril Rogers, who was the first to see many of the new mutations when they were introduced into the UK, two Violet cocks were close-ringed with Budgerigar Society rings in 1933. Curt af Enehjelm of Copenhagen wrote in 1940 about his experiences breeding Violets in the preceding 10 years. Many leading breeders took them up, but it was F. Garvey who established the most notable strain. Unless evidence to the contrary is forthcoming, it seems that the "Garvey strain", with its distinctive, deep, rosy hue has died out.

Perhaps the irony for those who admire Blue Budgerigars the world over, is that there is not a trace of blue pigment in ANY Budgerigar. It is all a trick of the light, which is broken up as it passes through small air bubbles sunk deep in the barbs of the feathers.

The objective of the authors* of this book – and the other books in the *All about . . .* series is to offer a platform for some of the world's most successful breeders of particular Budgerigar varieties to reveal their techniques, methods, likes, dislikes and hopes for the future. We believe we have succeeded. The experts have not been "led" when answering the comprehensive range of questions put to them and editing has been kept to the minimum required. After studying their answers, readers might like to look for the reasons behind each expert's success.

Inevitably, you will read more about Skyblues than Cobalts or Mauves. This is because this book is not based on theory but upon the practical experiences of fanciers who have enjoyed success at the highest levels. The fact is, notwithstanding fine wins that have been notched up by a few outstanding Cobalts there are many more good Skyblues benched at the top shows and it is rare to see an excellent Violet or Mauve on the show bench these days.

You will not find the colour standards or scale of points of any organisation – for more than one reason. Different countries have different standards. There is a distinct possibility that an international standard could be agreed before the end of the century. If you want to read a particular club's standards you can join the club – the space in this book is better devoted to the opinions of the breeders who have proved their ability by winning at the very highest levels. Colour standards and points allocations vary, but an outstanding Budgerigar is recognised the world over.

**(Roy Stringer, formerly a design engineer in the motor industry, is Features Editor of CAGE & AVIARY BIRDS. Fred Wright, once a teacher, is now freelance avicultural consultant to several companies and a regular contributor of articles to the same weekly journal. Both are successful champion breeders and exhibitors of Budgerigars and international judges.)*

Harry Bryan looks back

■ *Harry Bryan is the most successful Budgerigar fancier the world has ever known. He began keeping Budgerigars in 1916 and, in 1993, is still enjoying success on the show bench. In the intervening years he saw all of the top Budgerigars in the UK which until recently, in Budgerigar terms, meant the world. His memory is as keen as ever and here he recalls names from the past and some from the present; the top breeders of Blue Budgerigars of their time.*

In 1922, when I was 15 years old, I went to work as an improver at a hairdressers in Leamington Spa. The owner of the shop knew I had kept Budgerigars from the age of nine and so he introduced me to Mr King, a customer who had a similar interest, if on a much larger scale. He was very wealthy and lived at Eathorpe Park where he maintained an aviary. On my day off I used to cycle to the Park to see the birds. The aviary must have been 200ft long by 100 ft wide (61m x 30m) and contained a great flock of Budgerigars. Among the many hundreds of youngsters produced in 1922 there were two Blues; the first I had ever seen.

Blue Budgerigars were very rare in those days and most people's only chance of getting one was by buying Green split Blues. We know now that pairing two Green split Blues together produces a proportion of Greens that do not carry the Blue factor. However, knowledge of the genetics of colour expectations was not very great in those days and so many of these pure Greens were sold with the assurance that they were capable of producing Blues. At that time, I bought Greens which were claimed to be split Blue but they never produced a Blue.

From the time that Blues became more freely available I can recall several notable fanciers. Amy Brown, from Croydon, was one of the first to have Blues in the UK and she did a fair amount of winning for a time. Walter Higham was a top fancier who employed Len Hillas as his aviary manager and his Blues became well-known. The first Blue I owned came from Mr Higham. Major Tillotson, from Yorkshire, had the best Blues for most of the 1930s.

More recently, Fred Garvey, of Blackpool, was unbeatable with Violets for a 10-year period, but Violets were quite small in those days. Improving Mauves is a frequent ambition of newcomers to Budgerigar breeding, but I cannot recall anyone who has been successful in specialising with them. I can remember a few Mauves which had a pleasing pinkish tinge to their feathers. Even at the height of their popularity, no fancier had more than a few Mauves and they seem more scarce than ever these days. The favoured way of producing Mauves was to pair Cobalt with Cobalt and although I have tried this pairing several times over the past 10 years I have not produced a single Mauve.

I have bred a few good Blues myself over the years. One season I bred two outstanding Violets from large parents. The best died at the age of four months when a Sparrowhawk crashed into the wiring of my outside flight. The other was second-best Budgerigar at the Budgerigar Society Club Show in the 1970s. Perhaps the best Blue Budgerigar I have ever seen was one bred by Ike Flanagan, of Liverpool. It remained unbeaten for three years. Derrick Bowley, one of the experts in this book, did very well at the BS Club Show with an excellent Skyblue hen. Also featured are Gren and Pat Norris who have an excellent record with Blues, including winning the best in show and the best breeder at the BS Club Show, in recent years.

Today, although a few outstanding Blues are to be seen, they tend to be few and far between. The progress of the variety has been slowed down because Light and Dark Greens are not as good as they used to be. In the old days, Light Greens were so prepotent that we could pair them to Blues with confidence that they would bring about an improvement. Nowadays, Greens are just not good enough. A great opportunity awaits anyone who takes up the challenge of improving Blue Budgerigars.

("The Budgerigar Man", the Harry Bryan story and way of breeding exhibition Budgerigars is available from the publishers of this book)

MEET THE EXPERTS

DERRICK BOWLEY lives in the small country village of Hilton, in Derbyshire, England, though his native county is Devon. He kept his first Budgerigars at the age of 14, in 1938. The young Derrick exchanged his pet mice and rabbits for the Budgerigars; a common enough practice among children in those days. From the first time he saw a Skyblue Budgerigar he was entranced by it and when, in due course, he saw Cobalts and Violets he was utterly captivated. He has enjoyed many fine moments with his Budgerigars but two memories will always stay with him: his first win in a full class at Wolverhampton in 1953 and winning his first prize cards at the Budgerigar Society Club Show in 1955. He still treasures those cards. Much success followed and his greatest thrill came when a Skyblue cock of his own breeding took the best in show award at the 1977 Budgerigar Society Club Show, from what was a record entry for the time. The same Budgerigar had taken the Blue challenge certificate at the 1976 event and returned in 1978 to take a third challenge certificate. It is believed that this is the only Skyblue ever to become a registered champion by winning three CCs at the BS Club Show. As well as benching best Blue at this show on several occasions, Derrick has taken the awards for second best breeder in show, best opposite sex breeder twice and best opposite sex in show twice. Photographs of his Blues have appeared in the Budgerigar Society handbook and his 1977 winner can be seen on the cover of the one issued in 1984.

BRIAN BYLES lives at Banstead, in Surrey, England. The school which he attended had a Young Farmers' Club and, because he missed the animals when he left, he started to keep birds. Since 1950 his name has figured among the winners of major Budgerigar prizes. From the start he was fascinated by Normals but a special interest in Blues was initiated by the offer of a particularly good Skyblue cock from Ole Gade of Denmark. It had been bred by Maurice Finey, famous for his Normal Budgerigars. Although the Skyblue was lacking flights in one wing, it produced 35 chicks, with four hens, over a period of 18 months. Not one of them displayed feather faults. Three of his major wins in 1992 were with Skyblues; two best champion breeders and one champion any age. Over the years he has also taken many prizes with Light Greens. When he went to South Africa in 1973, with Alf Ormerod, the BS of SA had to change its rules to enable them to judge the National Championships. Since then he has judged in the USA, Brazil, Germany, Denmark, Holland, Switzerland, in South Africa on several more occasions and has admired the local Budgerigars during visits to Australia and New Zealand. Brian is well known as the Editor of *CAGE & AVIARY BIRDS*, the only weekly avicultural journal in the world, with a circulation of around 40,000. All of his friends keep birds and he would still be in the hobby even if his work was not associated with them. He rates himself lucky in having a job which involves his hobby.

GREN and PAT NORRIS are a husband and wife partnership who live in the East Anglia region of England. Gren has always had a liking for Blues and when several useful Blue Budgerigars began to appear in the nests of other colours, it permitted the Norris's to put more emphasis on the variety. This process began to take shape in 1985 and just four years later, Blues from the Norris stud were sweeping all before them. At the 1989 Budgerigar Society Club Show their young Skyblue was best breeder in show and best in show, while one of their Cobalt cocks was third best champion breeder and an Opaline Skyblue hen took a breeder challenge certificate. They notched up a notable double when another young Skyblue cock was best breeder at the same event in 1990, while the best-in-show winner of the previous year took the any age challenge certificate. Gren and Pat continued their successful progress at Budgerigar World Show taking best breeder with a Skyblue cock in 1989 and best in show with another in 1992. Their other successes with Blues are too numerous to mention. Pat (then Pat Baldry) started the ball rolling when her Skyblue was best breeder in show at South Essex championship event. (Before their marriage, the partners scored many successes under the name "Norris & Baldry"). Four years running, their Blues have taken best-in-show awards at the South Midlands Area championship. All together, at area championship events, the Norris's have taken – among other awards – five best in shows and 15 challenge certificates; all with Blues. At other championship shows, they have notched up 15 best in shows and more than 35 challenge certificates.

JOE SABELLA is a paediatrician who lives in Ridgewood, New Jersey, USA. Ridgewood is located in the north of the state, about 12 miles from New York City. Joe started in Budgerigars in 1953, but not in the United States! At the time he was studying Medicine at the University of Bologna, in Italy; one of about 100 American students there at the time. Due to his circumstances, he was limited to four breeding cages. The demands of his studies caused him to give up after two years. Back in the United States, he began again in 1971 with stock acquired from a few American breeders who had studs based on Alf Ormerod's bloodlines. Later, he was to introduce outcrosses from Jim Moffat and Chris & Arthur Snell; well known for their top-quality Normals, particularly Greens. Joe bred his two best Budgerigars in 1981 and 1982. They were both Skyblue cocks, reckoned by many to be ahead of their time. They were massive yet displayed excellent type and feather quality. Between them, these Blues took best in show awards in Maryland, New York, Connecticut and Eastern Pennsylvania shows in 1982/83. From 1984 until 1989, most of his wins were gained with Greens. However, these were split Blue and it was inevitable that top quality Blues would appear sooner or later. Since 1990 very high quality Blues have appeared so that the best Budgerigars in the Sabella stud are now Blues; mainly Skyblues but also Cobalts and Violets.

CHAPTER 1

THEIR BIRDROOMS

Describe your birdroom.

Derrick Bowley:

My birdroom is 20ft long by 8ft wide and 8ft-6in to the apex of the roof (6.1m x 2.4m x 2.6m). The roof overhangs the front wall by 2ft (61cm) and this serves as protection from both sun and rain. The structure – made from tongue and groove timber – is raised 12in (30cm) above the ground to permit cats to pass underneath. Because we live in the country there are field mice to be considered. I have found them in the garage but never in the birdroom. The room is lined with ½in (12mm) thick board, faced with white melamine, which provides excellent insulation. There are two double-glazed windows in the roof (each 24in x 18in (61cm x 46cm)) which give better light than the side windows. The door is in the centre of the front wall, with windows either side. I find sliding windows safer than hinged ones. There are two inside and two outside flights; each measuring 8ft x 3ft (2.4m x 0.9m). My discussions with other breeders suggest that breeding results from Budgerigars that have access to large, outside flights are no better than those from birds which are kept in smaller, inside flights. Even so, I prefer outside flights and Budgerigars go out in them in all weathers except fog. Budgerigars that can withstand the elements must be fit. Outside flights sort out the sickly ones. I will do everything in my power to save a sickly Budgerigar, but I will not breed from it. I have 36 breeding cages, 28 of them on the back wall. All have removable slides to create long flight cages which connect to the inside and outside flights. There is a 12in space below the lowest tier of cages (with sliding doors) which is used to store nest-boxes and the like. To one side of the door is a further block of eight cages, on wheels for easy cleaning. After the breeding season these become training cages for youngsters. My breeding cages are 24in long x 16in high x 18in deep (61cm x 41cm x 46cm). Each cage front has a 3in x 3in (7.6cm x 7.6cm) door which gives access to the outside nest-box. After studying many types and sizes of nest-boxes I now use outside boxes which measure 4½in square by 9½in high (11.4cm x 11.4cm x 24.1cm). When I used larger nest-boxes I noticed that the cocks spent long periods in the box and that many second and third-round eggs were infertile. With my design of box the hen fills the whole of the small concave and – although I get my share of clear eggs in the first round – infertile eggs in later rounds are practically unheard of. My cages and boxes are interchangable so I can move pairs with chicks to create bigger flight cages as the breeding season comes to an end. My room has few mod-cons. I

Thc overhaning roof of Derrick Bowley's birdroom gives shelter to anyone waiting to go in and prevents rain from entering the open windows. The interior layout (below) is ideal for serious Budgerigar breeders of any status.

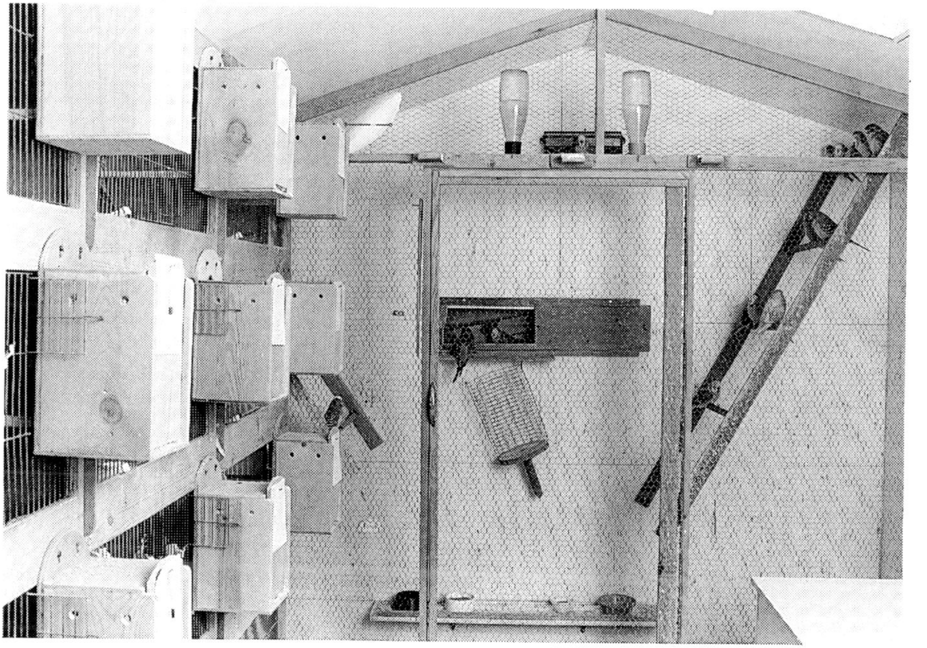

have two 100w bulbs on a time switch and two 15w bulbs as nightlights. Two ionisers keep the air fresh and two *Vapona* strips kill moths and flies. I admit to being old-fashioned and although I am willing to try anything beneficial, I do not instal gadgets for the sake of it.

Brian Byles:

My birdroom is "L" shaped with the length of each leg being 37ft (11.3m) and 34ft (10.4m). Each is 10ft (3.0m) wide. It is constructed from 3in x 2in (7.6cm x 5.1cm) framing covered with timber cladding on the outside and plywood on the inside. The gap between is filled with insulating material. It has a wooden floor, the main part on concrete piers and a later extension straight onto concrete. The roof slopes – but the wrong way! As arranged, rain cascades into the flights. The front walls are fitted with 3ft x 3ft (91cm x 91cm) windows for their full length. They are double-glazed units, but they are arranged so that the windows can be opened when the weather is hot. There are roof windows, but these too were a mistake. It is extremely difficult to stop them leaking. Ventilation is provided by a partially covered wire door, the opening windows and a series of small 6in (15.2cm) deep sliding "windows" along the length of the room, immediately below the roof. The best breeding results come from the pairs closest to these "windows". I have two large 9ft x 10ft (2.7m x 3.0m) outside flights which had to be reconstructed because some of their framing was rotting. I am not convinced that Budgerigars need outside flights but, as I have the space, I feel that the birds should have the opportunity to go outside if they wish. There are three inside flights. Two measure 12ft x 10ft (3.7m x 3.0m) and the third – used for sales birds or babies – is 10ft x 3ft (3.0m x 0.9m). Large inside flights are more important than outside flights as the birds have to be kept in during the winter and at other times when the weather is not good enough for them to be let out. Most fanciers provide insufficient inside flying space for their Budgerigars; not taking into account that good breeding seasons can result in overcrowding. There are plywood breeding cages along the back wall of the original section and all-wire cages opposite them – leaving a gap of 4ft (1.2m) between the two. This section also includes working surfaces, a sink unit and water heater. The rest of the birdroom is devoted almost entirely to flights. Thirty-six of my breeding cages are built in blocks of three on the Alf Ormerod design, with just a fixed rail at the front and a removable wire front. Each block is 8ft long by 16in high (2.4m x 0.4m). My other 18 breeding cages are of all-wire construction, measuring 36in x 18in x 18in (91cm x 46cm x 46cm) and made from rolls of 1in (2.54cm) x 1in x 16 swg *Twilweld.* The door is positioned in the end so that 18 cages fit in a 10ft section of the room. Nest-boxes fix onto the top right hand corner of the breeding cages and are made of plywood. They have a door in the front, held closed by two clips. The extra clip is a precaution as good chicks have been lost in the past when a door has fallen open. If the parents get out, eggs and chicks soon become cold. Equipment includes 3ft tubular heaters, time

Although Brian Byles is not convinced that exhibition Budgerigars need to go outside, the L-shaped configuration of his birdroom is ideal for incorporating large exterior flights. Inside the birdroom (below) both conventional and all-wire cages are employed.

switch and dimmer, fluorescent lights, ionisers, extractor fan (it is too small, I could do with a larger one) and an electric water heater. I also have a deep freeze in the birdroom in which I store corn on the cob. This luxury may have gone by the start of next breeding season as it is impossible to store enough to get right through the breeding season and not all my birds eat corn on the cobcob. It could well be better to buy bags of frozen corn every week.

Gren and Pat Norris:

We are currently using two birdrooms; Pat's original 12ft x 11ft (3.7m x 3.4m) room and Gren's 16ft x 8ft (4.9m x 2.4m). These will be changed for a single, much larger structure when time permits. Both rooms are made from timber, have wooden floors and are mounted on building blocks. The roofs are flat and covered with felt. Each has double windows and an extractor fan for ventilation control. We have only one flight (11ft x 5ft x 6ft-6in high (3.3m x 1.5m x 2.0m)) and that is internal. Inside flights are more secure and permit better environmental control. Our future birdroom will have much more flight space; all internal. The flight is situated in the smaller room along with nine breeding cages which can be converted into three 6ft (1.8m) long flight cages. The larger room has 32 breeding cages, along the whole length of the back wall, and a block of six cages at one end. The cages are 24in x 16in x 16in (61cm x 41cm x 41cm) and there are sliding dividers which can be removed to form flight cages of various sizes. The cages have storage space beneath. A cupboard is used to store equipment and its worktop is used for show preparation. There is a block of four training cages adjacent to the worktop and a conventional wire nursery cage which can be dismantled when not in use. All our nest-boxes are of the external type and constructed of ½in (12mm) thick plywood. Their external measurements are: 9in long x 6½in wide x 6½in high (22.8cm x 16.5cm x 16.5cm). The top of each box is divided into two; one half fixed and the other forming a hinged door. The hinged end slopes down at an angle of about 30 degs to give a reduced height above the sitting hen. We feel that the sloping roof promotes a feeling of security for the nesting hen as, in the wild, most hole-nesting birds lay their eggs at a point where the roof slopes towards the floor. Deep concaves are used, supplemented by plenty of wood flakes. Overall, our set-up is simple and very basic. Electricity is connected to both rooms. Lighting – fluorescent tubes and low-wattage nightlights – is controlled by time switches. Automatic emergency lighting is provided in case of a mains failure. Neither room is heated, but both are well-insulated. Running water is not laid on though we plan it in our future birdroom. Internal and external security devices are fitted to both rooms. In the main breeding room, humidity is controlled at 70 by an electrically-operated humidifier. Summer temperatures are controlled by reversible extractor fans and portable fans are employed if it becomes too hot. Plenty of spare 13 amp sockets are available.

At present, Gren and Pat Norris use two birdrooms. In the future they intend to build a much larger, single structure. The neat interior layout (below) includes well-built breeding cages and a useful nursery cage.

Joe Sabella:

My birdroom is typical of those used by Budgerigar breeders in the north-eastern part of the United States. It is located in the large basement of my old Victorian-style home. This poses two problems; lack of natural lighting and generally poor air circulation. The lighting problem has been offset to some degree by illuminating the entire area with *Vitalight* fluorescent tubes; the closest available to the spectrum of natural light. I have two small windows that have ¾in (18mm) slit openings to permit fresh air to enter. The size of these openings is enlarged considerably in spring and summer. The room is kept reasonably fresh by a large, electronic air cleaner (*Tectronic*) which provides some degree of air circulation and does an excellent job of clearing the air of moulted feathers and dust. The aviary is composed of three rooms. The main birdroom is 20ft x 10ft (6.1m x 3.0m) and houses a large flight; 11ft 6in x 5ft x 7ft high (3.5m x 1.5m x 2.1m). It is constructed from plastic and aluminium, the only wood being the perches. This flight (and a duplicate in another room) was made for himself by Fred Karch, a champion Budgerigar breeder who was in the plastics industry. I bought them after Fred passed away suddenly at a bird show in 1977. The main room also contains 21 breeding cages, 12 of which are 33in long x 19 ¼in high x 15in deep (84cm x 49cm x 38cm). The rest measure 25½in long x 16in high x 11½in deep (64cm x 40cm x 29cm). My nest-boxes are externally mounted and measure 12in long x 9in high x 6¾in wide (30.5cm x 23cm x 17cm). They are equipped with two blocks which fit inside; one with a concave. The blocks sit on top of a frame of timber which permits a shallow tray of water to be placed under the concave, to increase the humidity within the nest-box. This room is also equipped with a moveable cart and a seed bin. The main room communicates, via a door, to a 50ft long, 8ft wide (15.2m x 2.4m) corridor. This houses two small flights; each measuring 4ft long x 4ft high x 3ft wide (1.2m x 1.2m x 0.9m). These give barheads adequate space after they have been removed from the breeding cages. Most birdrooms I visit have nest feather youngsters in small, crowded cages. I feel that this is an unhealthy environment. The corridor leads to another room which is equipped with two flights. One the same size as that in the main breeding room and the other measuring 8ft x 4ft x 7ft (2.4m x 1.2m x 2.1m). A refrigerator, in this room, is used to keep seed mixes and nestling food cool, particularly in warm weather. Regulation of temperature is no problem because the house's main heating furnace is in the basement. My birdroom is kept at 70 deg F (21 deg C) in winter and between 75 and 80 deg F (24 – 27 deg C) in summer. From June to September many of the Budgerigars are transferred to another basement room which connects, by means of a window, to an outside flight; 12ft long x 8ft wide x 10 ft high (3.7m x 2.4m x 3.0m). The appearance of my birdroom is not ideal and I have plans to make changes in the future. My friends jokingly call my birdroom, "Catacomb Aviaries".

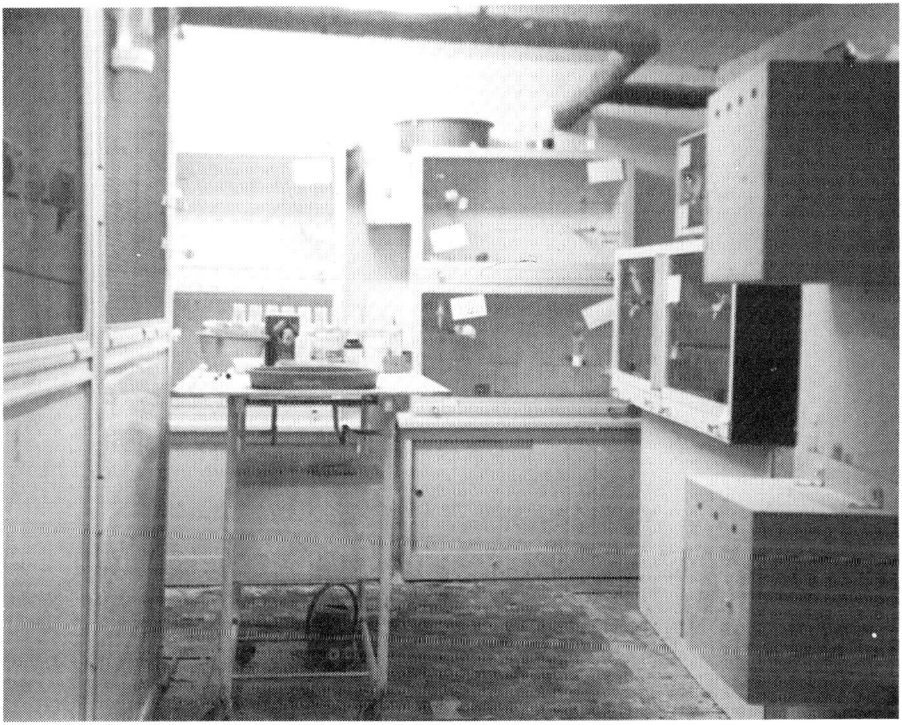

There is no exterior view of Joe Sabella's birdroom, it being housed in the basement of his home. The main breeding room (above) is well equipped and good use is made of a 50ft long corridor (below).

CHAPTER 2

MANAGEMENT

Describe a typical day's activity in your birdroom during the breeding season.

Derrick Bowley:

Method and organisation are essential in any birdroom and I pride myself upon being methodical. I normally check nest-boxes once a day, in the morning. The only exception is when eggs are due to hatch or to make sure that a newly-hatched chick is being fed. With 36 breeding pairs I can tell at a glance what is happening in every box without unduly disturbing the birds. A record card is attached to each nest-box with the blank face outwards. When the hen enters the box (I can tell by the disturbed sawdust) the card is turned round. Each egg is marked and recorded as it is laid. Note is made of whether an egg is fertile, addled or broken. If, after four days, an egg is found to be infertile, it is removed to persuade the hen to lay more; possibly fertile. It does not always work, but some of my hens have laid 12 eggs with the last five being full. In such circumstances it is best to foster the fertile eggs because I have known hens to smash these later eggs due, no doubt, to incubating for so long. When a chick hatches I hang a closed ring on the box to remind me it is there. I try to ring the chicks in a nest with consecutive numbers so if there are four chicks I hang four rings on the box. It also helps to avoid forgetting to ring a chick. I once missed ringing an outstanding youngster and this method ensures that it will never happen again. Every two days, each chick is checked to make sure that its ring moves freely and that there is no food clogged in the upper beak. If a hen looks a little off-colour I check to make sure that eggs and chicks are warm by holding them to my lips. If they are cold, I warm them in my hands and move them to another nest. Many a cold chick has been revived and cold eggs gone on to hatch. I always make time to inspect the non-breeding stock every day. My feeding routine takes about two hours a day. Water is changed every day in summer and every two days in winter. Once a week I clean out the breeding cages. I find the odour of the large droppings offensive and, to prevent the birds suffering, I remove these more frequently. I do not worry unduly about removing sawdust and chaff as I do not want to disturb the birds any more than is necessary.

Top left: Derrick Bowley
Btm left: Joe Sabella
Top right: Gren & Pat Norris
Btm right: Brian Byles

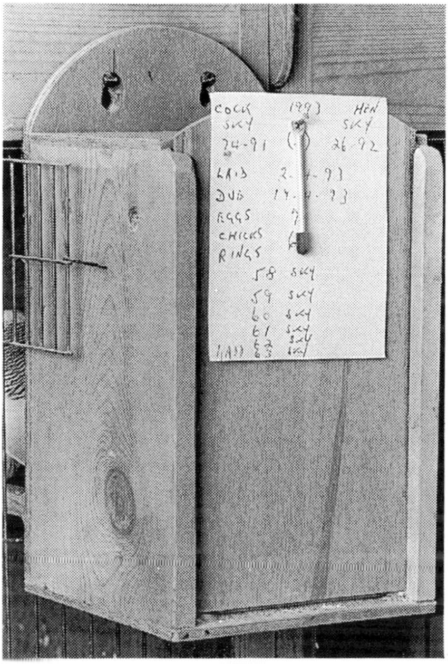

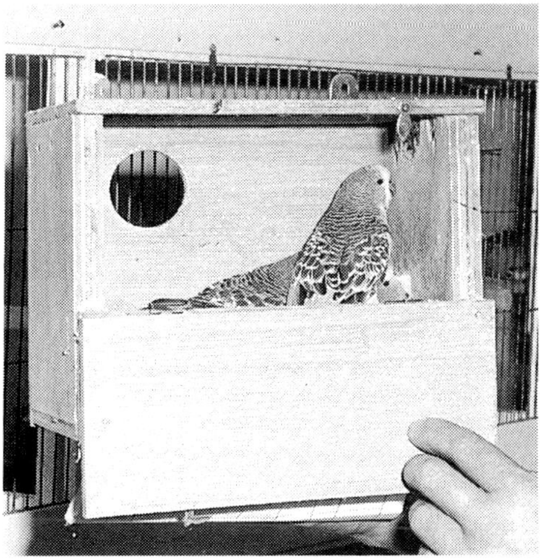

Four successful breeders; four nest-box designs. Derrick Bowley goes for extra depth, Joe Sabella incorporates a water dish beneath the concave to aid hatchability, while the Norris partnership and Brian Byles opt for the more conventional.

Brian Byles:

Before going to work I check the nest-boxes. Pairs with chicks are given soaked oats. Each evening, all birds are given hard-boiled egg and carrot, put through a mincer, and soaked oats. About once a week they also receive corn on the cob or sprouted mung beans. Drinking water is changed every other day, with additives being given to a selected programme. All nest-boxes are checked, eggs and chicks recorded on breeding cards. Concaves and sawdust are changed once a week when there are chicks in the box. Wooden cages, which have sawdust on the floor, have copious droppings removed daily. More thorough cleaning is carried out once a week. It is easy to remove sawdust and replace it with a fresh supply. Nest-boxes and adult birds are removed while this is done. I usually try to fit in some of the cleaning jobs during the week so that there is not too much to be done at week-ends. Seed pots are sieved, feeding boards washed, drinkers soaked in a solution of *Virkon S* for 15 minutes, floors are washed (every other day) and cobwebs brushed away.

Gren and Pat Norris:

At 8am each morning, Gren takes the softfood to the birdrooms and gives a finger drawer full to each pair. Those with chicks are given two or even three. At 12 noon, Pat gives softfood to the pairs with chicks. It is at 7.30pm that the main feeding and watering takes place. The droppings are removed from the breeding cages as feeding takes place. After that, the room is swept and tidied. Then, Pat checks the nest-boxes; recording eggs laid, chicks hatched, chicks ringed and any other happening that relates to a breeding pair. These records are transferred to the main stud register as time permits. One day each week, Pat washes and disinfects all the drinking vessels, cleans the windows and floors and vacuums both birdrooms. The flight is cleaned twice a week and the cages at least once a week.

Joe Sabella:

I maintain a fairly busy medical practice so the time I can devote to chores is limited. I awaken at about 6.45am each morning and by 7.30 I am in the birdroom. I prepare nestling food and go about first-feeding the breeding cages. I usually start by putting up about 10 pairs and gradually increase this number to 21; the limit of my available space. In any case, I doubt if I could manage many more because, unlike some other breeders, I do not have the time to care for 40 or 50 breeding cages. In my opinion, even the breeders who put up 40 to 50 pairs have only 15 to 20 which are capable of breeding the high quality of progeny at which they are aiming. The rest are fill-ins which consume a lot of time, increase the seed bill and crowd the aviary. After feeding the birds in the breeding cages I feed those in the flights. They all receive the same food. I then check the nest-boxes. I candle

A plastic ice-cream container is ideal for confining chicks during nest-box inspections; as demonstrated by Derrick Bowley.

Brian Byles' method of attaching nest-boxes with picture hangers makes it possible to lift them down for a closer inspection.

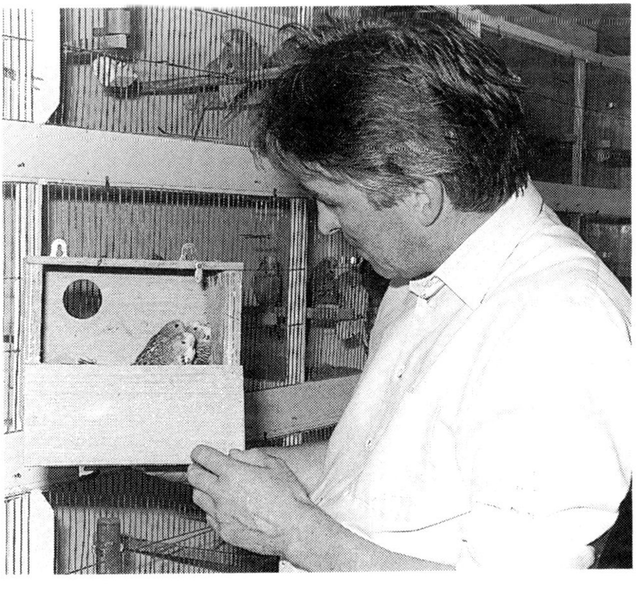

the eggs after the third has been laid though, if a hen is the nervous type, I wait until she is out of the box before checking. Any eggs that are transferred are marked with a felt-tipped pen. I use a code letter and a number, so B12 indicates that it was laid by hen B on the 12th of the month. Chicks are checked for growth, development, malformations and whatever problems arise with chicks. After 5pm, I change the water in the drinkers. The target is every day but sometimes, due to lack of time or ambition, I skip a day. My medical office communicates, through my consultation room, to the basement so if I have a free moment during the day I am able to check the birds. I check for such problems as chicks not being fed or chicks being abused. It is a tremendous advantage to be able to check on your breeding Budgerigars several times during the day.

Describe the activity in you birdroom during the lead up to a show.

Derrick Bowley:

As the show season approaches I pay a lot of attention to the youngsters; looking for likely show exhibits. As possible winners emerge they are placed in stock cages, usually with an older bird to steady them down. I attach a show cage, containing a millet spray, to the stock cage as I go about my birdroom duties. When an inquisitive youngster goes into the show cage I close the door for 10 or 15 minutes to get them used to it. This is repeated several times before they are placed into the cage individually and introduced to the judging stick. The birds are sprayed every three days; the last time being two days before a show. I use a powerful spray which leaves the birds looking bedraggled. Any dirty marks on their heads are washed using soap and water, cotton wool and a toothbrush. Care is taken to wash all the soap out and to make certain it does not go in the eyes. Masks are trimmed two days before a show. I never remove tail feathers. I have done it before and the feathers never regrew. I work on the principle that if they miss one show there will always be another. When de-spotting a bird I occasionally find it has less body weight than I like and it is kept at home. It is better to be safe than sorry. It is advisable to have more than one reserve available as Budgerigars have a nasty habit of dropping spots and tails at the most inconvenient time. When choosing which shows to exhibit at, I have to check that they fit in with my judging engagements. The Budgerigar Society Club Show, Midland Budgerigar Association and my local Trent Valley B&FBS are important to me. About three weeks before the show I study the schedule to check patronages, nominations, entry fees and the like. Entries are made with the appropriate fee and a stamped, addressed envelope. As the show approaches the show cages are washed, inside and out. When I receive the cage labels I write the numbers on a separate piece of paper. To avoid mistakes, after putting in seed, I place the bird in the cage and then stick on the label. Not too long ago I put the labels on first and managed to wrong-class an excellent Skyblue hen. If your bird is in the wrong class you are beaten before you start.

Brian Byles:

I am not a keen exhibitor and exhibit at few shows, so I am not very methodical as far as this side of the hobby is concerned. I never remove broken feathers in an attempt to get a Budgerigar ready for a particular show, but I do feel that it is a good thing to give possible exhibits plenty of spraying. I tend to lose interest in Budgerigars as exhibits after they have been shown for a season and prefer to compete with young birds. I do not like exhibiting hens because I believe that their best place is in the breeding pen. I would hate to "spoil" a good breeding hen by exhibiting it. After I have selected the show team, I wash any that have dirty heads. I spray them a couple of times with warm water and a final time with cold water, two days prior to the show. I trim masks over two or three evenings rather than attempting to deal with all of the birds in one go. It is better to go back a day later to finish trimming a mask rather than rushing it and pulling out a wrong spot.

Gren and Pat Norris:

Every morning, the weather is assessed and if the forecast is for a hot day, ventilation is increased and additional portable fans are brought into use. The show team and any potential show birds are housed in flight cages according to sex and age. For example, young birds are housed separately from old birds. The object of caging is to increase weight and to steady youngsters. Broken flights are removed though broken tail feathers are taken out only when they come away easily in the hand. The point at which the tail feather enters the body is always supported during this operation. Spraying of birds takes place two or three times a week; generally in the early evening. Any birds going into a major moult are removed and placed in the flight. Each Monday, we take note of the classes in which we have entered birds for our next show. In most cases, several birds of each colour, age and sex will be prepared for show, though this depends upon the choice of birds available. The show team receives intensive spraying both morning and evening, right up until the day before the show. We do not believe in light spraying so our Budgerigars always get a thorough soaking. Any with pin feathers receive extra attention. They are brushed gently with an old toothbrush and warm water to open the feathers. Multi-spotted birds have some additional spots removed during the week but the final mask trimming is not carried out until the day before the show. No special preparation is used to enhance the birds' plumage, other than plenty of clean water. Any birds that show signs of blood after despotting or the brushing out of blood quills, are washed with cold water and baby shampoo. This may have to be repeated several times if bleeding persists. Surplus water on the feathers is soaked up with a paper tissue. On occasions it has been necessary to repeat this performance on the morning of the show; just prior to caging up. The show cages are prepared – with seed and labels – the evening before the show. No bird is sent to a show unless it is in tip-top condition and will do itself – and us – justice.

Joe Sabella:

A basic show team of about 10 to 20 Budgerigars is selected prior to the show season and any broken feathers are carefully removed. I may exhibit at eight to 10 shows each season but the one that is most diligently prepared for is the "All-American"; staged in late summer/early fall. I do everything possible to have my best birds ready for this show, but I limit the show team for other shows to the birds that happen to be in decent condition. About two weeks before a show I give each show bird a thorough soaking with luke-warm water. They are then placed in show cages until dry. After that they are sprayed with cool water every two or three days and, again kept in show cages until dry enough to be returned to the flights. I have tried adding various substances (glycerine, liquid soap, vinegar, etc.) to the spray water but have never seen any difference from using plain water. About four days before the show, excess mask spots are removed and any pin feathers are stroked gently with a dull (blunt) hacksaw blade.

CHAPTER 3

FEEDING

How do you feed your Budgerigars?

Derrick Bowley:

Basic seed mixture:

Where feeding is concerned, I work on the principle of letting my Budgerigars eat what they like. In my early days I used to put a seed mixture in the hopper and soon found that certain birds liked certain seeds – and threw the others on the floor! Some liked millets. Others liked plain canary. I tried forcing particular seeds on Budgerigars and discovered that, if they did not like them, they preferred to starve than eat. All foods are now offered in separate pots. When I worked at a brewery in Burton-on-Trent I was told that barley was purchased from different places because they contained different percentages of moisture, protein and fats. So I buy a mixture of canary seeds that come from different countries. My Budgerigars have access at all times to plain canary, mixed millets and Budgerigar tonic seed. I add extra oats to the tonic because the birds like it so much.

Extras:

I feed carrot every other day, millet sprays (cut into pieces) every day and *Maxi-feed* or *Smithwain* in a finger drawer once a week. When I lived in town I grew luscious chickweed on my allotment and my Budgerigars loved it. Now I live in the country I am afraid to collect it in case it is contaminated. Before I retired, my birds were fed any time between 8.00am and 10.30pm. Now they are fed regularly at 9.00am, though I have to confess that it has made no detectable difference. During the breeding season I start feeding softfood seven days before the first chick is due to hatch. It consists of oats and mung beans soaked in water for 48 hours then thoroughly washed and drained. These are mixed in a basin with *Haiths* Protein food and half-a-teaspoonful of brewers' yeast. Whenever I walk down the garden path, stirring this mixture, the birds become excited. To check whether they have a sense of smell I tried stirring an empty bowl. The birds were not fooled. When I put the mixture in the bowl they knew it was there, even though they could not see it. I repeated this test several times; always with the same result.

Drinking water:

I put boiled water in the drinking fountains. I keep a gallon container in the kitchen and when a kettle is boiled to make tea, whatever is left is put in the container. This also ensures that water is cool before being offered to the

A solidly-constructed seed bin, such as the one in Derrick Bowley's birdroom, is easily built at very little cost - and with the lid closed it serves as a seat.

birds. The water in my area is very hard and in the 1950s I suffered a lot of dead-in-shell. The egg shells were very hard. A Canary breeder advised me to boil the water and I get very few dead-in-shell now. I once expounded this theory while giving a lecture and an expert maintained that boiling the water would not help. All I can say is that I believe it works for me.

Additives:

I have tried various tonics over the years but never found them to be beneficial. Now I never put additives in drinking water unless a bird is ill.

Grit and minerals:

Grit, cuttlefish bone and mineral blocks are always available. When my birds come back from a show they ignore the drinkers and millet sprays and go straight to the grit pot. I mix mineralised grit with oystershell at a ratio of 4:1. This is fed in test tube feeders. It is easy to see when they need refilling though, in any case, they are changed every 10 days. The grit that my Budgerigars preferred best came from a Scottish beach; collected at ebb tide and allowed to dry. I think the salt content made it attractive.

Brian Byles:

Basic seed mixture:

At this time I am using *Trill* but in the past have used English-grown plain canary seed and mixed millets. When separate seeds are offered they are put in different dishes in order to discover just how much of each is being consumed.

Extras:

Hard-boiled eggs, carrots and bread crumbs are used as softfood throughout the year. I am impressed at the results that Jo Mannes has been getting and feel that his success is due, in no small part, to the animal protein his Budgerigars get from hard-boiled eggs. Soaked clipped oats, sprouted mung beans and millet sprays are offered though the sprays are given mainly to chicks and birds that are off-colour. Most fanciers do not take into account the way that Budgerigars have changed since they were brought in from the wild. The extra size and feather they now carry means that they need better feeding. I am sure that most breeders would experience better results if more animal protein was fed. Budgerigar breeders need to experiment more. Why not try some of the different forms of livefood which are normally only given to insectivorous species?

Drinking water:

My Budgerigars receive filtered tap water.

Additives:

Entrodex (probiotic) and vitamin/mineral supplements (all produced by *Vydex Ltd*) are used throughout the year added either to the drinking water or softfood. I tend to use less rather than more than the recommended amount.

Grit and minerals:

Several different types of grit are given; limestone, mineralised, etc. plus cuttlefish bone and mineral blocks. Powdered cuttlefish bone is also added to the eggfood once or twice a month.

Gren and Pat Norris:

Basic seed mixture:

We make up our own seed mixture comprising: 3 parts English plain canary, 3 parts Canadian plain canary, four parts mixed millets and one part condition seed which is made up of equal parts of small sunflower, linseed, niger and hemp. The seed is washed in a solution of *Vanodine V18* (10lbs (4.5k) of seed at a time), drained and dried for three to four days prior to feeding. Up until 1988 we always fed the above mixture but then – due to pressure of work – we changed to a commercial seed mixture. This coincided with two disastrous breeding seasons. We took stock of the situation and changed back to our original seed mixture and seed source. Since then, we have seen a notable improvement in both breeding performance and general condition. We feel that the mixture we give provides both variety and balance, It offers seeds rich in oils, vitamins, carbohydrates and protein.

Extras:

During the breeding season our pairs receive softfood, in small quantities, twice a day. When not breeding, it is given to them once a week. Softfood consists of Pat's own preparation: 1 hard-boiled egg (mashed finely), 2 digestive biscuits (reduced to crumbs), half a teaspoon of natural wheatgerm, half a teaspoon of *MVS30* (multivitamins), a quarter teaspoon of *Protamin* and a pinch of salt. This is added to an equal quantity of soaked groats. This mixture provides a good blend of easily digestible, natural foodstuffs; containing a broad spectrum of protein, vitamins, minerals and carbohydrates. *Maxi-feed* is fed in finger drawers; every day to breeding pairs and once a week to the rest of the stock. Owing to the difficulty of obtaining a clean source of chickweed it is no longer fed. Our Budgerigars now receive carrots once or twice a week throughout the year, corn-on-the-cob when in season and an occasional apple. Soaked millet sprays are fed to all breeding pairs and chicks that are being weaned. A piece of soaked millet spray, placed in the nest-box, encourages chicks to start feeding themselves and keeps the hen occupied while she is brooding. All of the foodstuffs, supplements and minerals we give our Budgerigars are in a natural state and the birds are permitted to decide what their own requirements are.

Drinking water:

Clean water is given every day, directly from the tap.

Additives:

The only time any additive is used in the drinking water is when a hen lays a soft-shelled or porous egg. Soluble calcium is then added to the water until the condition improves.

Grit and minerals:

Cuttlefish bone, iodine nibbles and *Versel-laga* mixed grits are fed at all times. A cattle lick is available in the flight. These are replenished every two or three weeks. *Murphy's* minerals are given, in a finger drawer; at all times to breeding pairs and once a week to the rest.

Joe Sabella:

Basic seed mixture:

We really do not have adequate knowledge of how Budgerigars need to be fed so, to ensure that my birds receive as wide as possible a range of foods, I use a seed mixture that is very complex in its make-up. It is called *Abba 1600* and is made by Abba Products, Elizabeth, New Jersey, USA. It is composed of millets, plain canary, oat groats, shelled sunflower seeds, safflower, buckwheat, cracked corn, flax, sesame, hemp, peanuts, ground mollusc shell, wheat meal, soya bean meal, coconut, eggs, bone meal, beef, poultry, carrots, dandelions, chicory, kale, grapes, bananas, apples, oranges, pears, apricots, fish, honey, corn syrup, brewer's yeast, cod liver oil, beta carotene, wheat germ oil, dextrose, vitamin supplements A, D3, B12, B2, niacin, calcium and various mineral salts. I add two parts of *Abba 1600* to one part plain canary to form my basic mixture.

Extras:

During the breeding season each cage receives a nestling food called *Abba Green 92*, to which water is added to create a crumbly consistency. It is also fed daily, in small quantities, to the birds in the flights. *Abba Green 92* is basically the same as *Abba 1600* but with the seeds omitted. Its protein content is around 15 per cent.

Drinking water:

Unfiltered, fresh water daily. The water in my village comes from artesian wells and has been shown to be non-contaminated over the years.

Additives:

Protexin (a probiotic) is added to drinking water every other day. The concept of stimulating a bird's natural intestinal flora is appealing.

Grit and minerals:

A mineral mixture composed of oyster shell, mollusc shell, eggshell, sea sand, charcoal, bone meal, salt, potassium iodide, ferrous sulphate, copper sulphate, nickel sulphate, zinc sulphate, magnesium oxide, calcium phosphate and carbonate.

CHAPTER 4

MEDICATION

What do you look for when checking your birds' health and what do you do about it?

Derrick Bowley:

The trained eye can always spot a Budgerigar that is "under the weather". The inexperienced should look for birds that are huddled up in the corner of the cage, listless, puffed up, pumping their tails, with heads under their wings, have loose droppings or clogged vents. My vet has told me that warmth helps sick birds and I have often found the use of a hospital cage to be successful. A hen that is huddled in a corner could be egg bound. I treat this in one of two ways; either putting liquid paraffin on the vent area plus holding over steaming water (not too close!) or sprinkling table salt on the vent. The clogging on a vent should be removed gently with warm water and *Dettol* and not roughly pulled off. If in doubt about these or any of the other conditions mentioned, consult a vet, but make sure he knows something about birds.

Brian Byles:

Most experienced breeders can spot a sick bird as soon as they enter their birdroom. Knowing what to look for is only part of what is required; making sure you check every bird every time you enter your birdroom is even more important. If I find a sick bird, I place it in an old all-wire hamster cage, which also doubles as a spray cage. I fix towelling around the sides and place an infra-red heater above the cage, being careful to position it so that it keeps the bird nicely warm without getting too hot. The alternative is to place the cage on top of an electric heater.

Gren and Pat Norris:

A close watch is kept on our Budgerigars' health as part of the daily routine. At the first signs of a bird being fluffed up and having loose droppings, it is caught up and examined for weight loss, coloration of droppings and signs or smell of vomiting. If a bird shows signs of sickly smelling vomit it is dosed with a solution of *Mysteclin* in water, by syringe, directly into the crop. Vomiting without any smell is treated with *Trykil* (Emtryl soluble) as directed on the package. A bird with loose droppings is

Whether it is tube-feeding or administering medication, four hands are better than two. Here, Gren and Pat Norris demonstrate one of the benefits of a partnership.

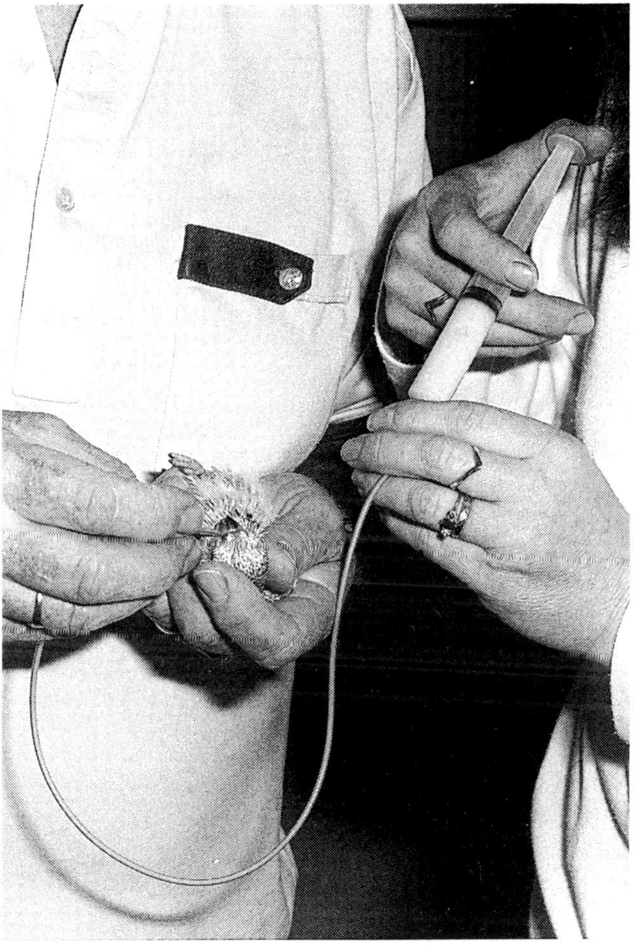

isolated and given cold tea for two or three days. If it does not respond, a sample of droppings is taken to the local vet for analysis and the bird is treated in the manner prescribed by the vet. Any fluffed-up Budgerigar is placed in a show cage and moved to a warm room. A variety of seeds and softfoods are offered to encourage eating. If a fluffed-up bird also shows signs of weight loss it is treated in the same way but a watch is kept on which seeds it is eating. Some Budgerigars, when transferred to a flight, are bullied and prevented from eating. Others eat only a particular seed, which may be available in only small quantities. If the condition persists and seed is being de-husked without being consumed it generally indicates that the bird is going light; a condition for which there is generally no cure. Sometimes an afflicted bird will eat plenty of softfood which leads to its recovery, but this is rare.

Joe Sabella:

Budgerigars that are quite sick are usually detected easily. They have characteristic signs: puffed up, matted feathers in the mask and head area, soiled or matted vent, hunched giving the appearance of a shortened neck. In many cases, the illness has progressed too far before it has become very obvious and, despite good treatment, the bird will never be the same again. So it is important to watch your Budgerigars for the first signs of illness (lethargy, dull eye, refusal to socialise). I pick them up and if there is no sign of a problem I continue to observe them. If a loss of weight is apparent ("going light"), I know there is a problem. I treat with a solution of *Ronidazole* 0.5% by dropper in the mouth; once a day for three days. In almost all cases the bird concerned perks up and feels well. I find *Ronidazole* fine for Trichomonas infections and also helpful in many other bacterial diseases. There is no problem of overdosing with this drug. Early treatment is important. Any delay makes illness in Budgerigars difficult to cure. For diarrhoea and clogged vents I use *Furoxone* (a Nitrofuran) which is a good treatment for E Coli which causes most cases of enteritis in Budgerigars. If diarrhoea does not respond to *Furoxone* after a few days I switch to an anti-fungal agent called *Nizoral*, which is used for humans and comes in a 200mg tablet form. I pulverise a pill and dissolve it in 1pt of the birds' drinking water. When treating a single bird I use a dropper to administer four drops daily. I know that the use of heat in the treatment of sick birds is widely practiced, but as I have never used it I cannot evaluate its effects. Recently, I have found a medication which is very effective for E Coli infections. It is called *Apralan* (Apramycin Sulfate). It is supplied in the form of a powder which dissolves readily in water (1 teaspoon to a gallon of water) given for eight days.

What does your birdroom's medicine chest contain?

Derrick Bowley:

Scaly face cream, liquid paraffin, clear iodine, eye ointment, *Vanodine V18*, *Dettol*, *Vaseline*, Terramycin, scissors, tweezers and ring cutters.

Brian Byles:

I have a couple of bottles of antibiotic which were given to me by Bob Travniceck from the USA. They are of a type not available in the UK.

Gren and Pat Norris:

Mysteclin, a syringe, scaly-face cream, witch hazel, scissors, a ring-cutting tool, calcium tablets, Epsom salts, *Trykil* (Emtryl soluble), *Ivomec*, *Lactade* and forceps.

Joe Sabella:

Neosporin (opthalmic ointment for eye discharge), *Ronidazole* (for trichomonas and possibly other infections), *Nizoral* (for fungal infections), *Furoxone* (for diarrhoea and clogged vents), *Ivomectin* (for scaly face), Apple bitter (to spray on heads of chicks that are being feather plucked), chloroform (to dispose of terminally ill birds) and nail clippers.

Do you use medication on a routine, preventative basis?

Derrick Bowley:

I have never considered giving routine medication or worming my Budgerigars.

Brian Byles:

I have used *Trykil* (Emtryl soluble) against trichomoniasis. I have also administered antibiotics, but only when necessary. I have never wormed my Budgerigars.

Gren and Pat Norris:

Our stock is treated with *Trykil* (Emtryl soluble) every six months and any new additions are treated before they are permitted to mix with the rest of the stud. Antibiotics are not given on a routine basis, but only to sick birds.

Joe Sabella:

I de-worm my Budgerigars at least two months before putting them down to breed and, sometimes, after the breeding season.

CHAPTER 5

THEIR STUDS

(Readers who are not conversant with the genetics of colour expectation will find it helpful to refer to Chapter 7 when the experts discuss pairings that produce Blues).

How many Budgerigars do you keep and what varieties are they?

Derrick Bowley:

I select which birds to retain (helped by my son, Geoff, who has an excellent eye for a Budgerigar) after the youngsters have moulted out. I retain 45 cocks and 75 hens with quality rather than age being the main consideration. Of the 120 retained, 110 are Normal Blues; the remainder being Greens, Pieds and Spangles. I have won the odd challenge certificate with the last two varieties. Opalines and Cinnamons are disposed of, regardless of their quality. It is my ambition to breed only Normal Blues but the odd Opaline or Cinnamon always appears. A few years ago, I reached chick number 200 - all Normal Blues - before Opalines appeared in the last few nests

Brian Byles:

I never count my Budgerigars. They probably total a couple of hundred. Although I do not keep a large number of Blues - perhaps around 30 - the ones I do retain are tend to be among the best of my stock. The rest of the stud is made up of Light Greens, Grey Greens and Greys in Normal and Spangle form. I also keep a few Opalines, Cinnamons and Opaline Cinnamons.

Gren and Pat Norris:

We keep around 160 Budgerigars and about half of them are of the Blue series. We also keep Light Greens, Dark Greens, Grey Greens, Spangles, Pieds and Cinnamons in both their Normal and Opaline forms.

Joe Sabella:

I keep between 100 and 175 Budgerigars, depending upon the time of the year. Numbers are at their lowest just before the breeding season. At present, my stud contains a higher proportion of Blues than in previous years. In the late 1980s I kept predominantly Greens. Most of them were split for Blue and Blues have taken over in the early 1990s. I do not get rid of a Budgerigar if it is a useful bird, no matter what its colour. Besides Skyblues, Cobalts, Lights Greens and Dark Greens I have around 12 Violets. I have Opalines, Cinnamons and Spangles in all colours and a family of Fallows (about 20) which I have been upgrading for the past eight years.

Which of the other varieties can improve your Blues?

Derrick Bowley:

I do not keep any other colour specially to improve my Blues, however, I am always prepared to use a very good Dark Green in order to maintain their depth of colour. I once borrowed a good Dark Green cock from my son Geoff having first checked that it was not split for Opaline. In the event, although it produced excellent Blues, it turned out to be split for Cinnamon and so produced Cinnamon hens. They were quite good and went to Geoff.

Brian Byles:

All of my Normals seem to display the same quality though, from time to time, one colour becomes prominent. All Normals seem to complement each other and can be cross-bred to advantage, although in recent years I have bred more Blues and Grey Greens than Light Greens and Greys. My efforts are all aimed at improving and maintaining the overall quality of the stud of Normals rather than concentrating upon and trying to develop a single colour. The elimination of opalescent markings and flecking takes priority in a Normal stud. I try to keep the Grey factor away from my Light Greens and Blues because of the possibility that it might have adverse effects on their coloration. If Light Greens or Skyblues lose some richness of colour, good, deep-coloured Dark Greens and Cobalts can be used to great advantage. Many years ago I discarded all of my Opalines – cocks and hens – so that I could concentrate on Normals. After a few years it became obvious that my stock had lost head qualities because I was no longer using Opalines. I have regretted this ever since. If one compares the head qualities of Normal hens as opposed to those of Opalines it soon becomes evident that Opalines have a definite place in the stud of a breeder who aims to produce good Normal Blues. These days I retain very few Opaline cocks but a lot of attention is given to Opaline (and Opaline Cinnamon) hens. If they are wide-headed, have good spots and do not carry any major faults, such as heavy flecking, they are retained and results indicate that they help head quality; particularly width of head.

Gren and Pat Norris:

Dark Green and Light Greens – both Normals and Opalines – can help to improve Blues. All our Green series Budgerigars can be traced back to a Light Green hen which excelled in size, feather quality (in both density and length) and was a natural show bird. This hen was paired with a large Cobalt cock and produced high-quality Budgerigars in both the Blue and Green series. The Dark Greens from this mating possessed great depth and evenness of colour and these have been used to impart the same colour qualities to our Blues. This is the reason that our Blues have become noted for their depth of colour.

Joe Sabella:

Varieties which can certainly improve Blue Budgerigars are Light Greens, Grey Greens and Greys. In my opinion, the old cliché about "dipping into the Greens" to bring about improvements still holds true. I also feel that a good Grey can breed a quality Blue. It is best to use a Grey that has been bred from a Blue. This, mated to a Blue, will produce a high proportion of Blues. It is difficult to improve a stud which contains only one colour or variety. I will use a good Budgerigar of any variety to improve another. At the time of writing, my Blues have been increasing in quantity and quality though their predominance is a matter of chance. In the early 1980s my two best Budgerigars were Skyblue cocks; massive, with excellent feather and ahead of their time. In the mid-1980s my best birds were Light Greens.

CHAPTER 6

ALL ABOUT BLUES

What is the attraction of Blues and is specialising a good idea?

Derrick Bowley:

It was by chance that some of my first Budgerigars were Blues, but in the early 1950s I saw Cobalts at a local show and became determined to have a shed full of Normal Blues, one day. Many people have favourite objects - a lady and her favourite dress, a cricketer and his favourite bat - and when asked "Why" can only reply: "I just like it." That is the reason I keep Blue Budgerigars. It gives me a tremendous thrill to walk into my birdroom and see large numbers of Blues flying around. I have three ambitions with Budgerigars: 1) to win the BS Club Show with a Blue I bred myself, 2) To be unbeaten in the Blue classes for a whole season and 3) to have the best stud of Blues in the country. I achieved No. 1 in 1977, I almost achieved No.2 when I entered 32 Blue classes and won 28 of them, but No.3 would be a difficult claim to make. I know I have a good stud of Blues. Even if someone could claim that they have the best Blues, that is still different to having the best stud. An advantage of specialising is that you should always be able to send out a full show team, even if a top-class bird drops its tail or spot. On the other hand, by not specialising you stand a better chance of winning more classes. I remember standing with Eric Lane watching the best-in-show judging at a big show. I was represented by the best Blue but he had six best-of-colours in the line-up. Eric took the top award.

Brian Byles:

Normals have always been my favourite variety and that means that my stud is incomplete unless it contains good Blues. Regardless of what colour mutations are available, Normals have that little extra attraction as far as I am concerned and although Blues are one of my favourites, who can resist the appeal of Greens, Grey Greens and Greys? Every breeding season brings its share of problems but breeding an outstanding Skyblue cock can make up for all the disappointments. A thing of beauty is a joy forever and what can be more beautiful than a Blue Budgerigar of quality? Few Budgerigar breeders are true specialists these days. How can they be when you cannot guarantee that a pair of Light Greens will produce all Light Greens or that a pair of Blues will breed all Blues? Trying to be too much of a specialist can result in a breeder cutting his own throat when he disposes of an outstanding Budgerigar which does not fit into his plans. Specialise by all means, but in Normals as a group rather than a single colour.

Gren and Pat Norris:

It was their beautiful coloration – particularly the dark factor forms – that first attracted us to Blue Budgerigars. In our eyes, nothing can beat the beauty of a large, well-balanced Skyblue or Cobalt displaying to best effect in a show cage and it is our intention to keep Blues to the forefront of exhibition Budgerigars. The challenge, for us, is to retain the colour quality of our Blues without losing any of their exhibition competitiveness. Our target for the future is to develop Mauves and Violets up to the same standards as our Skyblues and Cobalts. Specialising in Blues can be a problem in the early days of being involved in the Fancy as it is difficult to obtain sufficient numbers of the required quality to permit you to pursue your objective. Specialisation also limits the number of classes in which you can compete at shows. The time to specialise – if one so wishes – is when your stud has developed to a reasonable level of quality. By then, the breeder should have built up sufficient knowledge of genetics to use the qualities within the stud in a positive way; to bring about a rapid improvement in the chosen variety. Experience will also make you aware of the pitfalls which lie in wait for the breeder of that variety.

Joe Sabella:

As far as the attraction of Blue Budgerigars is concerned, I believe each breeder has his or her personal preferences. I am enjoying specialising and concentrating on Blues and am convinced that I can bring about big improvements. One drawback of specialising in the USA is that the main prizes go to the best 10 Budgerigars in show. An exhibitor who shows in several different classes has more chance of getting birds into the top 10. We watch the judges at work at our shows and so if your exhibits are limited only to the Blue classes your interest is diminished. So, in essence, I think it is best not to specialise in the USA, although the breeders who concentrate on one colour or variety will probably achieve more success with it.

What makes a good – and a bad – Blue?

Derrick Bowley:

A good Blue must, first of all, be a good Budgerigar, which means that it must be well-balanced. It is no use a Budgerigar having an excellent

"'Power' is essential", says Brian Byles. This is one of his powerful Skyblue cocks.

head if it is short in the body and has crossed wings. Once you achieve balance you can start eradicating minor faults. In my view, there is no such thing as a bad Budgerigar. They are like Scotch whisky. I asked a Scottish friend which was the best brand. He replied: "All of them! Though some are better than others." All judges have their likes and dislikes. As far as I am concerned the major fault is poor head quality. A good Budgerigar has width, backskull and uplift above the cere. When I was a novice, Harry Bryan told me that without a good head a Budgerigar is nothing. Crossed wings, a dropped tail, short mask with spots almost touching the beak and lack of backskull are also obvious faults. A good show bird must stand up boldly off the perch as if it is saying: "Look at me!"

Brian Byles

A top-quality "modern" Budgerigar must be large and have wide shoulders on which to carry its head and mask. If you lose width, you lose much of the "power" that is essential on a good Budgerigar. These features have been improved beyond recognition over the past few years. First-class deportment and feather quality also come into it, but you only have to study the top winners at major shows and it is the width across their shoulders and head which puts them above the rest. That applies to Blues as much as any other colour or variety but, with Blues, you also need deep, rich body colour. In my own stud, I give the same emphasis to any Normal whether it is Green, Blue, Grey Green or Grey. Except for those of raw beginners, no stud should contain Budgerigars with such really serious faults as narrow heads, poor deportment, bad wing carriage or dropped tails. It is a waste of time spending years trying to eradicate major faults so the aim should be to start with Budgerigars of a reasonably high standard.

Gren and Pat Norris:

In our opinion, a good Blue Budgerigar should possess certain essential features including:

1) Showmanship, style, deportment, call it what you will. We look for a Budgerigar that stands fearless on the show cage perch and cries: "Look at me!"
2) Head features. These should include width, backskull, frontal rise and blow but most important is depth of mask. A good Budgerigar with a short mask does not attract the eye, but an average Budgerigar with depth of mask demands that the judge takes a second look.
3) Good strong colour. This is a feature of our own Blues regardless of their shade. An illustration of this point is that, on several occasions, we have exhibited Mauves and they have been mistaken for Violets. A Blue without strength of colour has something missing. A Blue with depth of colour has a luminescent quality which attracts the eye.
4) As with any other colour or variety, a good Blue must also have type, size and shoulder, but features numbers 1) to 3) above are essential.

When it comes to the various faults that can afflict an exhibition Budgerigar we are in agreement. However, on which is the worst we disagree, so each offers our own list. Gren: 1) Lack of width of head, 2) Lack of feather and blow, 3) Short mask, 4) Nipped neck, 5) Bad backline (humped or dropped tail), 6) Poor colour, 7) Bad stance, 8) Lack of showmanship, 9) Opalescent markings, 10) Head flecking, 11) Small spots, 12) Lack of size. Pat: 1) Bad backline (humped or dropped tail), 2) Bad stance, 3) Nipped neck, 4) Short mask, 5) Lack of width of head, 6) Lack of size, 7) Lack of feather and blow, 8) Lack of showmanship, 9) Head flecking, 10) Opalescent markings, 11) Poor colour, 12) Small spots.

Joe Sabella:

The answer would be the same, regardless of the colour or variety under discussion. We all strive to produce a big Budgerigar with good head qualities, type, a deep, wide mask with large, round spots, a tucked-in beak, good backline and excellent feather quality. In other words, a Budgerigar which approaches the "Ideal". It goes without saying that a bad Blue would be deficient in these qualities. Another important factor for any colour is intensity of that colour. Is it evenly distributed or is it patchy? Blues that display dark, vibrant coloration are the best. It is possible to pick out the individuals with intense body colour and jet black markings, in the nest. One can detect the black coloration of their feet, claws and beaks.

Which faults are correctable and which are not?

Derrick Bowley:

I do not accept that there is any fault that cannot be corrected. With patience and time you can gradually eliminate any fault. It must be done a bit at a time by introducing Budgerigars that do not have the particular fault that is concerning you. There is great satisfaction to be gained from doing this. I sometimes receive letters asking for Budgerigars that are big and bold, have wide heads, deep masks, round spots, good backskull, excellent wing carriage, etc., etc. I frequently write back asking them to let me know if they find anyone with that sort of bird for sale so that I can visit him myself!

Brian Byles:

Most faults can be corrected – but why waste several seasons trying to correct faults when, by taking a little more care over the selection of your initial stock, it need not be necessary? Opalistic markings are a fault on Blues that can make the difference between a winner and an also-ran. It is a trait that is more prevalent in some families than others so care must be taken not to introduce the fault – or to discard the birds concerned if it appears – or it can spread through a stud, but then this can be said of all faults. I WILL work with a flecked bird as long as it is not lacking in any other respect, though it is pointless using a flecked Budgerigar if one of equal quality, with a clean head is available. I have firm memories of visiting Dr Alf Robertson in Durban, South Africa, when he was producing outstanding Budgerigars which could have swept the board in the UK. He gave me a Grey Green cock which had been best Budgerigar and best breeder at the BS of SA National Championships and when I exhibited it at London & Southern Counties BS Area Championships it took the best in show award. Many of his top birds, including Blues, were bred from heavily-flecked Opaline Green and Opaline Grey Green hens (most of which were split Blues) that had "bucket-shaped" heads. These came from pairings in which both cock and hen were heavily flecked. How he managed to breed so many fine, perfectly clean-headed winners from such pairings I do not know, but he did it for many years. He had obviously studied his stock and had learnt what they were capable of producing. If there is a lesson to be learnt from this it is to know your birds and how they will behave in the breeding pen. That applies to every aspect of selection and not just to flecking.

Gren and Pat Norris:

All faults are correctable – given time. Some are more difficult to correct than others and some appear later in life and grow worse with age. The most difficult faults to correct are: lack of width of head, nipped neck and (in Pat's opinion) a poor backline. Put in its most simplistic form, faults are corrected by ensuring that the breeding partner of a bird carrying a serious fault does not, itself, display the same fault and neither do its parents. The degree of difficulty of eliminating a fault depends, to some extent, upon how closely bred the stud is. When a major fault appears in a line-bred stud (such as our own) the majority of the stock will be carrying the fault in visible or hidden form, in the same way that the stud carries desirable features. Under such circumstances it would require the introduction of several outcrosses, from lines that do not have the same fault. Such an action would be a backward step and it could take many generations to restore the stud to its original standard of excellence. Anyone intent on line-breeding must do everything in their power to ensure that the original stud birds do not carry any major fault, visual or hidden.

Joe Sabella:

It is only worth trying to correct a fault if, in other respects, a Budgerigar is good enough to be used in the breeding scheme. Faults that are correctable and worth correcting are: small spots, short behind the perch, smallness of stature and imperfect backline. Naturally, it is necessary to find a partner which does not have the fault in question or, even better, excels in the feature you are trying to correct. If you have enough Budgerigars without faults it would be better not to increase the workload by breeding faulty ones. Budgerigars that are decisively narrow in the head, pinched in the neck, have shallow masks, poor wing carriage (dropped or crossed), dropped tails and display poor colour are best eliminated from the breeding programme except for use as feeders. It is too time consuming and difficult to try to correct such faults which will, in any case, reappear in future generations. A fault that I can personally tolerate (though there is room for discussion) is opalescence on Normals.

What do you think are the strengths of your own stud? Are there any features that you would like to improve? What do you think of other breeders' and other countries' Blues?

Derrick Bowley:

The strength of my stud – and of course I am biased – is its good, all-round standard. I set a standard and retain nothing below that level. Some breeders have a few really good Budgerigars but the rest are of a much lower standard. I do not believe that such a collection merits being called a stud. I believe that complacency is the first step on a downhill path and so I would like to improve EVERY feature of my Budgerigars. I usually manage to keep my hens up to standard but the cocks are a little more difficult and I have to pay a lot of attention to maintaining backskull. Because I put so much stress on it, colour depth does not pose many problems. I have visited many world-famous studs in my time and made many valued friendships. So when it comes to praising other breeders' Budgerigars I must maintain the principle of discretion being the better part of valour. I would hate to hurt anyone's feelings by omitting them by a slip of the pen. My impression of overseas Blues is based purely on what I have been told by other fanciers. From this it would seem that Blues abroad are well behind the standard of those in the UK. Of course, there are good Blue Budgerigars overseas, but it would seem that there are not many of them. Being realistic, Budgerigars have improved so much in recent years that my BS Club Show winner of 1977 would be beaten by the Blues that have taken the top awards over the past few years.

Brian Byles:

I am not sure that my own stud has any strengths. I do not have a Budgerigar which, in my opinion, does not need improving in some respect. In most, I would like to see more size, better deportment and richer colour. At present I am trying produce birds with more width across the head and shoulders. Budgerigars that were good enough even a few years ago are now dropping behind because they do not have extensive width of head and shoulders. Most of us struggle for year after year to breed a few good Budgerigars. Some seasons are better than others but, very often, we take two steps forward and one step back. The strength that most of us have is the determination to succeed, if not one year then, maybe, the next. In the history of the Budgerigar Fancy, a handful of breeders have put themselves above the rest: Harry Bryan, not only for his outstanding success on the show bench for so long but also for his constant determination to win even now when he is in his 80s; Dr Alf Robertson, of Durban, South Africa, for having, in his time, a stud of exhibition Budgerigars which was second to none despite not having access to outcrosses such as we in the UK have (there was an importation ban in South Africa for several years); Ken Farmer, whose Budgerigars were outstanding but who always gave buyers a square deal (I now regret not buying Budgerigars from him in the 1950s when he offered them to me at bargain prices); Alf Ormerod whose skill as a breeder of top-quality Budgerigars will be long remembered. More recently I have been amazed at the outstanding Budgerigars being bred by Jo Mannes in Germany and Jorge De Pina in Brazil. Each has reached the top in different ways. Jo has an inbred stud, whereas Jorge has suceeded by outcrossing. Until recently, Britain was said to have the best Budgerigars in the world, but so many top Budgerigars have been sold abroad that fanciers in some countries have been catching up and - in a few cases - have overtaken us. As far as Skyblues are concerned, I do not think any country has a lead on the UK, the exceptions being the outstanding Skyblues that can be seen in numbers in the Mannes and De Pina studs. Such is the progress that has been made in recent years that it is hardly worth comparing the Budgerigars of today with those of yesteryear. Even the Opaline Dark Green that took the supreme award for Harry Bryan in 1957 would be regarded as a pet today. The Joe Collyer Grey Greens were probably the first big step towards the development of the "modern" Budgerigar. Their offspring went to the studs of Harry Bryan, Maurice Finey, Alf Ormerod, Mrs Angela Moss and others. In my opinion, we are seeing in Jo Mannes' stud a further development of the modern Budgerigar. He has used top-quality Budgerigars, bred by the likes of Alf Ormerod and Jim Moffat, and has used his skill to build up a stud of Budgerigars which are individually and collectively superior to those seen elsewhere. I also believe that a mutation has taken place which enables him to breed Budgerigars in numbers despite their size and quality. Mannes is the German equivalent of Alf Ormerod and has many of his characteristics. He is clever enough to understand feather quality and knows how to improve it.

Gren and Pat Norris:

The features of our Budgerigars which attract most comment from visitors are head quality (mask, backskull, width and blow) and showmanship. We feel that we could improve on head feather density, particularly lateral density, and backline is a feature that is receiving more attention of late. We admire Derrick Bowley's Blues. Although he is not keen on Buff feathering he has managed to bring together all of the essentials of top-quality show Budgerigars, including size. Jo Mannes' Budgerigars are now among the best in the world and we have never seen such quality of feather in such quantities in a single stud. Our only first-hand experience of overseas' Budgerigars has been in Germany and the best Budgerigars there are every bit as good as those in the best UK studs. Today's Budgerigars are superior to those of previous decades. You only have to look at photographs and film of yesteryear's winners to appreciate the truth of that. Even so, comparisons of birds and breeders of the past is more difficult than it sounds. When Gren came into the Fancy, 43 years ago, the exhibiting of Budgerigars was much more localised and some breeders with top-quality stock never ventured more than 20 to 30 miles from home. For this very reason, we doubt if many people will remember Wilf Smith of Peterborough, yet he had wonderful Budgerigars whose feather qualities were superior to most others of the time. It was Wilf who showed Gren the first family of flecked Budgerigars he ever saw. They were being used to improve spot size and length of feather of the rest of the stud. Other names, most from the past, whose Budgerigars have left a lasting impression are: Norman Horne (Northampton), Brian Carter (Kings Lynn), Peter Osborne (Kings Lynn), Jim Healy (Peterborough), Harry Renshaw (Spalding) and Bill Bancroft (of Sutton-in-Ashfield and still going strong in partnership with his wife Lyn). Norman Horne's Budgerigars always had showmanship bred into them. Peter Osborne's Yellowfaces had wonderful faces and blow, Brian Carter's Budgerigars had tremendous shoulder and size. Jim, Harry and Bill had the ability to pair together average-looking Budgerigars to produce top-class specimens. Budgerigars which have left a lasting impression are: the wonderful Dark Green cock which took best in show at the BS Club Show for Alf Ormerod and Doug Sadler, Mr & Mrs T. Howitt's Opaline Cinnamon Skyblue cock which took best intermediate any age at the BS Club Show and two Budgerigars that 99 per cent of the Fancy never saw. These were a Yellowface Skyblue cock and a Skyblue cock, brothers owned by J. Collison of Norwich. Either of them were capable of figuring in the BS Club Show specials.

Joe Sabella:

As far as Blue Budgerigars in the USA are concerned, I am familiar with most of those in the north-eastern part of the country. Don Langell has had some excellent Blues. Francis Curran has some of the best Cinnamon Blues around. Al and Dennis Lalavee, of New Jersey, have excellent Blues. Crawford Maddux, of Texas, had an excellent Skyblue cock that was second best in show at the All-American in 1991. In recent years, the general quality of Blues in the USA has not been as good as Normal Greens. I believe that my two Skyblue cocks of the early 1980s were better than any that are around today. On the foreign scene, some of the Blues I have admired in the UK are A. Gibbons' Skyblue cock (best Blue at BS Convention '90), G. & P. Norris's Blues and M. & K. Richmond's Cobalt cock that took best in show at the 1992 Budgerigar Society Club Show. I have also admired Jorge De Pina's Blues, in Brazil, but have seen them only in photographs. However, the most incredible Blue Budgerigars I have ever seen were those I saw when I visited Jo Mannes in Germany in 1991. I do not believe there are Blues of equal quality anywhere in the world. They were simply the best. As far as my own Blues are concerned, I would like them to have bigger spots - without running into head flecking problems. In general, they have excellent head width, but I would like to see even more of this. I have a Skyblue cock in my aviary, hatched in 1992, which I believe could compete well, world wide. I would also like to instil more style and showmanship into my Blues. It is distressing to have a superbird in the flight, only to see it act awkwardly and not display its true worth when placed in a show cage.

What is the best way of breeding a good Blue?

Derrick Bowley:

What a question to ask! The theoretical answer would be by studying pedigrees. Thankfully, this does not always work in practice – or it would mean that the well-off could succeed the best. I once knew a Pigeon flyer who enjoyed moderate success with his own bloodline. He went out and bought the best Pigeons money could buy, paired them with his own and his results were even more moderate. Their blood did not mix. I realise that I limit my own chances by refusing to pair Opalines and Cinnamons to my Normal Blues, no matter how good they are. This is because my single objective is to breed a good stud of Blues, and only Blues. In a mixed stud I can see the advantages of using Light Greens, Dark Greens, single-factor Greys or, if you can get one, a really good Mauve. I am fortunate in having a son who can lend me a good Light Green or Grey which I use for one season only. When checking pedigrees, if I find that a bird has been bred Skyblue to Skyblue for three generations, I make sure to pair it with a Cobalt. Skyblue x Skyblue for too long risks losing depth of colour. There are always differences of opinion about the boundaries between inbreeding and line-breeding. A well informed friend of mine maintains that any pairing which involves mating blood relatives is inbreeding. Suffice it to say that I have paired an exceptional parent with one of its progeny – and been disappointed with the results. I have enjoyed much more success by pairing cousins and even Budgerigars that have a common great-great-grandfather.

Brian Byles:

Breeding good Budgerigars is usually a hard slog. There is far more to it than just selecting the right pairs. To start with, the Budgerigars selected need to be able to breed. Otherwise, making pairings – even if they are the best in the world – is a waste of time. I believe that there is a need to use a combination of inbreeding and outcrossing. Inbreeding brings the good features together and establishes them. Outcrossing prevents a stud becoming so closely bred that it loses its propensity to breed. Let a stud get too close and its fertility drops, hatchability levels decline and even the size of the Budgerigars that you do manage to breed gets smaller. If you breed only with unrelated stock it becomes a lottery; a matter of chance whether the good points come together on one bird. As I see it, there is no set way to breed good Budgerigars. All breeders – even the successful ones – have their

A nursery cage on wheels is a valuable piece of equipment. This one increases chicks' confidence and gives Derrick Bowley the opportunity to study another year's crop of youngsters.

own methods. Some get by with luck and few stay at the top for long. I have seen my own stud decline because the birds became too closely bred. From a very good pair of Alf Ormerod Grey Greens I bred two or three outstanding youngsters in 1971. Ten years later, every Budgerigar in my stud had them as ancestors and results began to decline. Quality went down and breeding results became worse. An infusion of new blood is now helping to improve matters. The question of how close one should breed is impossible to answer. Most people answering this question would not take into account matings which have been made over the years. Two Budgerigars may not be, say, brother and sister, half-brother and half-sister, but look back five or 10 years and you find that they have common ancestors. Most champions who have been breeding for a decade and more will have inbred studs, unless they keep an extremely large number of Budgerigars and bring in large numbers of outcrosses. I like to keep families together, but I have learnt that there is a need to introduce outcrosses on a regular basis. When it comes to the finer points, you need to take into account the features which judges find to be important; for example mask spots. I have sometimes been accused of being "spot mad" but I have always had Budgerigars with large spots; a throwback to the Ormerod and Finey birds upon which my stud was based. Controlling the shape of spots is more difficult because it depends upon the shape of the feather which a Budgerigar is carrying. If the feathering becomes wider or longer, it affects the shape of the spots. With Blues, good depth of colour is essential; more so in Cobalts and Mauves than with Skyblues. As with spots, feather quality has a great influence on colour. It is much easier to achieve good colour on finer-feathered Budgerigars than on Buffs and double-Buffs. Alf Ormerod maintained that the colour of Skyblues can be improved by pairing with deep coloured Cobalts and Dark Greens. Features such as spots and colour need to be controlled right from the start by a policy of vigorously discarding any bird that does not come up to a predetermined standard. Life will then be much easier later.

Gren and Pat Norris:

Before setting out to breed a good Blue Budgerigar you need to establish, in your own mind, what the essentials of the variety are - and then appraise your stud to make sure that these features are present, even if they are carried by non-Blue birds. Pairings which we have found to be very effective are Skyblue x Skyblue, Skyblue x Cobalt (our favourite pairing), Light Green/Blue x Cobalt or Skyblue and Dark Green/Blue x Skyblue. If one of the partners happens to be an Opaline we do not worry, as long as the pairing is right in every other respect. The pairings we mention retain the depth of colour of our Blues. Conversely, any pairing that introduces the Grey factor has a detrimental effect on colour intensity and so Greys and Grey Greens are avoided when breeding for Blues. Occasionally, a Cinnamon Blue appears in the nest of one of our Blue pairings and this is retained in the family as we have not found any problem in loss of colour when it is paired back with a Normal. From time to time we have paired a Spangle with a member of our Blue family but have been disappointed with the quality of the chicks produced on every occasion so we no longer use this pairing. Dominant Pieds have also been used and the results have been much more encouraging. Many of our pairings are made with the future in mind and so we do not expect to produce exhibition quality from some of them in the first generation. However, we have worked out that the progeny will be beneficial in the next year's planning - or even the year's after that. An example of such a pairing is one where we would expect to breed outstanding head qualities while accepting a loss in body length and style. Those missing features will be introduced over the next couple of years and so this approach is well worthwhile. We never pair together two Budgerigars that both lack head quality or are both short in the mask. When it comes to

Brian Byles' birdroom, in its pleasant garden setting, is well protected by trees. (photograph: Les Lockey)

This bold Skyblue cock, from the Byles' stud, excels in head quality. (photograph: Les Lockey)

(above) Blues, Blues and yet more Blues. Derrick Bowley examines a nest of Blues while others look on from an inside flight. (photograph: Les Lockey)

A super young Skyblue hen from the Bowley stud. (photograph: Les Lockey)

This outstanding Skyblue cock took the best breeder in show award for Gren and Pat Norris at the 1990 Budgerigar Society Club Show. (photograph: Les Lockey)

This 1991-bred Skyblue cock demonstrates the quality of Joe Sabella's Blues. (photograph: Joe Sabella)

The face, mask and head of this very young Norris Skyblue cock suggest that the partners have bred yet another winner. (photograph: Les Lockey)

Derrick Bowley believes in crossing his Skyblues with Cobalts at regular intervals to maintain their depth of colour. This Cobalt cock is good enough to stand on its own merits. (photograph: Les Lockey)

Joe Sabella bred this excellent Skyblue cock in 1992. Among its other good features, it excels in size. (photograph: Joe Sabella)

This super Skyblue cock, bred by Brian Byles, needs another week before it will be ready to go to a show. (photograph: Les Lockey)

Top of the world! This superb Norris Skyblue cock was best breeder and best in show at the 1989 Budgerigar Society Club Show. (photograph: Les Lockey)

A lovely Skyblue hen, bred by Derrick Bowley. (photograph: Les Lockey)

Another excellent Skyblue cock from the Sabella stud. (photograph: Joe Sabella)

It does not take an expert to detect the Buff feathering on this Brian Byles Skyblue cock. Large spots have always been a feature of his stud, a throwback to the Ormerod and Finey birds upon which it is based. (photograph: Les Lockey)

Gren and Pat Norris do not worry if one of the partners in a breeding pair is an Opaline. This Opaline Mauve cock (left) and young Opaline Cobalt hen (below) would help any stud. (photographs: Les Lockey)

A top-quality Skyblue hen from the Brian Byles stud. (photograph: Les Lockey)

Derrick Bowley has a knack of producing the sort of feather texture that wins shows without resorting to coarseness. This outstanding Skyblue cock illustrates the point. (photograph: Les Lockey)

relationships, our general practice is to line breed. Our favourite pairing is cousin to cousin and, in the case of important stock birds, we would pair grandfather to granddaughter or grandmother to grandson. Our reasons for line breeding is to impose dominance of our birds' best features. The grandparent pairing is used only when the older relation is an outstanding Budgerigar which displays a minimum of faults. In our opinion, line-breeding is the only way to maintain quality within a stud.

Joe Sabella:

The most important factor is that the parent birds complement each other. If I had a Light Green/Blue cock of excellent quality I would pair it with a Blue hen. Another good mating is a coarse-feathered (Buff) Skyblue cock with a long, wide-headed, tubular, fine or intermediate-feathered Blue hen. The hen would have to have a deep mask and good-sized spots. I do not think it is a good idea to pair Blue to Blue over a long period of time because, eventually, you will lose size. Opalines, Cinnamons and Opaline Cinnamons in Grey or the Green series can be helpful in producing top-quality Blues. The same rules apply to breeding a good Cobalt. I believe that dark-factor Blues can be just as good as Skyblues – as long as you are prepared to use your best birds in their production. To breed a good Violet you need to start with a Budgerigar which is carrying the Violet factor. A Cobalt or a Dark Green could be used as a mate, with the former giving a higher proportion of visual Violets. When Greens are used, there is the added problem of trying to detect which of the Greens you produce are carrying the Violet factor, so that you can plan a future Violet-breeding programme. Whatever colour you are trying to breed, you are liable to meet problems with large, Buff hens. They tend to lay eggs irregularly (if at all), fail to sit their clutches diligently enough to bring them to the point of hatching and, if they do, are poor feeders. When I have managed to get such a hen to lay and incubate she has often turned out to be a good mother. The best chicks of the season have often come from a hen like this. I think that timing (and luck) play a part in any mating being successful. I use hens of lower visual quality for breeding only if they have an excellent pedigree and, even then, do not pair them with my best cocks.

How would you advise a newcomer to Blues to set up a successful stud?

Derrick Bowley:

Building up a stud of Normal Blues takes a great deal of time, patience and – I must admit – a lot of heartsearching. If a newcomer wants to move up the ladder quickly they should buy the best stock available but – in my opinion – they would lose a lot of satisfaction. In my early days I had no ambition to become a champion in the least possible time. I was quite content to build a stud of Blues while enjoying the hobby and educating myself about Budgerigars. I prefer a more gradual approach and think it is best to go to an established breeder, who has a reputation for breeding good Blues, to buy between four and six pairs; of average quality, from good-class stock. From these you should breed a few that are better than their parents. Retain these and the parents that bred them and get rid of the rest. Never keep a Budgerigar purely out of sentiment. Then go back to the original breeder for a further one or two pairs. Following this procedure for a few years will build up the nucleus of a good stud of Blues. As the stud begins to show an overall improvement, you can think about buying Blues of much better quality, perhaps two a year – but it is easier to advise this than to actually find birds of the right quality. When you do acquire new stock ask the seller to let you have a few day's supply of seed and a bottle of the water which the birds are used to. These can be blended gradually with your own seed and water supplies.

Brian Byles:

I would not advise any newcomer to start with nothing but Blues. It is better to take a more general approach and to keep mainly Normals with a few Opalines and Cinnamons. As you begin to make progress with a number of varieties, you should be able to detect in which direction your progress is taking you. Unless money is no object, I would aim to start with six pairs and I would obtain these from two top breeders rather than rely on just one. In this way you keep your options open and have two bloodlines which can be brought together at a later date. Obtaining the initial stock from one breeder makes you more reliant upon him. His birds could be all you require but, on the other hand, they may fail for any number of reasons. I would pick two top breeders and stick with them. My first good stock came from Maurice Finey and Alf Ormerod. Both had good Budgerigars but they had different characteristics and were bred in different ways. Alf brought in outcrosses on a regular basis. Maurice did not do this to anything like the same degree and, as a consequence, his stud was more inbred. Back in the 1960s, I bought a trio of Budgerigars (one cock and two hens) from Alf Ormerod. The cock, an Opaline Grey, was very vigorous. In the course of 12 months I had him paired with the two Ormerod hens and two of my own. All produced good chicks and helped me to build up a family. So buying a good trio is another way of making a start, if money is limited.

Gren and Pat Norris:

The first requirement of anyone wanting to set up a winning stud of Blue Budgerigars is patience – unless they have a bottomless pocket! If we needed to start again we would adopt the following method: We would look for fanciers who were winning with young birds in Normal and Opaline

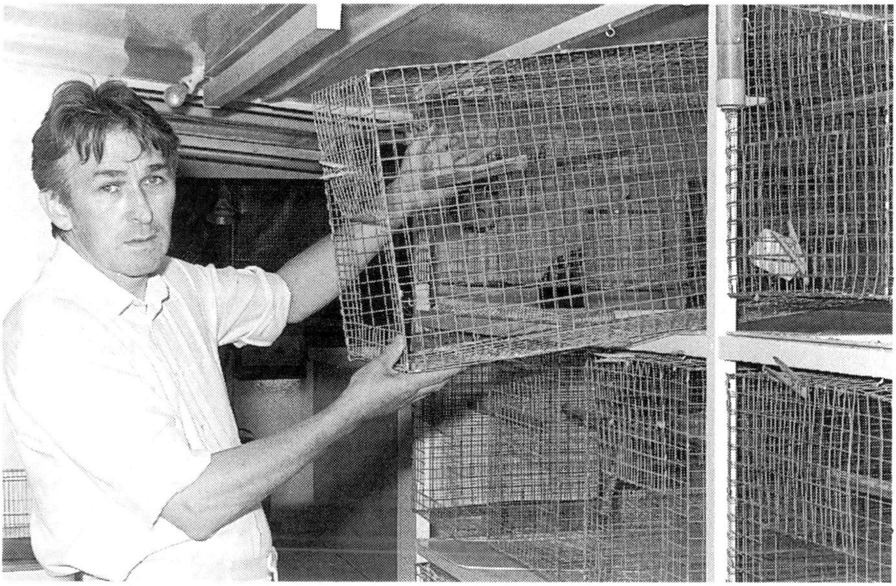

Brian Byles has found them to be so useful that he is considering changing over entirely to all-wire cages. Here he is seen removing one to be cleaned by hosing down.

classes. At this stage, colour would be unimportant. We would visit them to find out which were practicing line-breeding. We would then set out to buy eight to 10 pairs from up to four different sources. We would not be trying to buy top-class show specimens but their lesser (much lesser) brothers, sisters and cousins. The physical characteristics of the parents and the grandparents of the birds we were buying would be far more important than those of the birds themselves. Having said that, they would have to display some visual quality and not be rubbish specimens. Within the birds we bought, we would try to include all of the main features that, together, make an outstanding exhibition Budgerigar – even if the features were spread across all of the birds. For the first breeding season we would pair together related birds which complemented each other – taking into account the features of their parents. In a later round we would interbreed the unrelated birds obtained from different studs. In one season we would have in-bred and outcrossed. At the end of the breeding season we would assess the youngsters to find where the best ones had come from and to find which parents had demonstrated dominance in passing on their features – both good and bad. In the latter case, both parents and offspring would be discarded. If any of the desirable features had failed to materialise we would need to go out and obtain further stock. In the second breeding season we would make progress because we would know which birds were dominant for good features and could pair accordingly. Closely related pairings would be made and others which incorporated the previous year's outcrosses. As years progressed, more and more good features would become evident on the youngsters and what had started as three unrelated families would have become our own line. If any feature was seen to be diminishing it would be corrected by bringing in new blood which excelled in that feature. Once the standard of the stud had been fixed, colour specialisation could be given greater emphasis by pairing together birds of the appropriate colour or ones which are split for that colour. This would increase the numbers of the colour and we could then start concentrating on such factors as depth and evenness of colour.

Joe Sabella:

I would advise a newcomer to join a Budgerigar club and to make friends with successful breeders. He should go to area shows and meet other breeders. He should visit aviaries and learn how to assess a Budgerigar correctly. It is impossible to select correct pairings, and so make progress, unless you have developed an eye for a Budgerigar. This takes time and effort. I would advise buying about six pairs of Budgerigars from two breeders and six of the 12 birds should be Blues. They should be no more than two-years-old and of a quality that the breeders are prepared to let go for a small amount of money. Advice should be sought (and followed) on the best way of pairing them and an effort should be made to understand the reasoning behind the advice. When chicks are produced, the newcomer should not only make his own evaluation of their quality but also ask an experienced fancier (perhaps the seller of the original pairs) to assess them. Something should be learnt by comparing the assessments. The best Blues and the very best of the non-Blues should be retained. Each year a further three Budgerigars could be introduced; one from each of the original breeders and one from a new source. With patience and careful selective breeding, more and more Blues will be good enough to be retained – always remembering that a very good Budgerigar of any colour will be useful. A newcomer should read all available material and try to understand how the genetics of colour expectation work.

How important is it for you to ring chicks at the earliest possible time?

Derrick Bowley:

Early breeding means very little to me. The fitness of my Budgerigars determines when I pair them and this generally means mid-January. With luck, chicks emerge in the third week in February when the days are getting longer. I once varied from this because my birds were bouncing with health in November. I paired them and had the worst start to a breeding season I have ever suffered. The chicks from my second round have always matured as well as those from the first, by the time the BS Club Show comes around. Some people wonder how I can quickly recognise which chicks are from the first round and which from the second. It is not because I have a wonderful memory. The fact is that until the end of April 1 ring on the left leg and any that hatch after that are ringed on the right leg.

Brian Byles:

It is a long time since I took into account the date that closed rings are issued. When Maurice Finey was selling up I managed to get one of his best Budgerigars; a Skyblue cock. It was not only three years old but also a Buff-feathered bird with most of the flight feathers of one wing missing. That Skyblue was paired up in September and produced full eggs. Because of this success, since then, I have always tried to breed from awkward Budgerigars during the autumn months. This idea has gradually caught on and now I plan to pair up as many birds as possible in September. Breeding good Budgerigars is more important to me than showing.

Gren and Pat Norris:

The ringing date for chicks is of no importance to us. What IS important is to obtain chicks from pairs that are ideally suited and such pairings seldom coincide with ring-issue dates. Quality is our first concern - irrespective of the time of the year.

Joe Sabella:

The ring issue date in the USA is (as in the UK) January 1. I do not agree with that date. It is very difficult for a young Budgerigar to compete with an older one until late in the year. Our shows begin in April and run until some time in November. A Budgerigar that wins a best breeder award at an early show will have done so against very little competition and its quality may not be worthy of such a prestigious prize. In some cases it is a waste of time making the award. Years ago the fine-feathered birds that were in vogue quickly reached maturity but, as the exhibition Budgerigar has progressed to its present high standard, it has taken longer to attain its full potential. I would like to see this recognised by bringing the ring issue date forward to November 1.

How do you go about acquiring stock of the required quality?

Derrick Bowley:

The availability of good Blue outcrosses is very limited. There are good Blues around but their owners, quite understandably, do not wish to part with them. So I try to exchange with someone who is using my own bloodlines. Just what a friendly hobby this is was brought home to me in 1991. My Budgerigars are not used to any outside noise as my birdroom adjoins open fields. One day diggers, earth-movers and bulldozers started work within feet of my birdroom. I lost 32 Normal Skyblue and Cobalt hens with broken necks, prolapses and stress. I was devastated. I will not name names, but I was given birds – many of my own bloodline – with no strings or conditions attached; six from Lincoln, three from Cambridge, three from Leicester and two from Lancashire. I was given a wonderful Cobalt hen that I had judged the previous year. I declined offers of Opalines and Cinnamons but was nevertheless very grateful.

Brian Byles:

Fortunately, I have a few friends who are prepared to exchange birds. If you can work with other breeder in this way, you can often acquire a better quality bird than would otherwise be the case. I was also fortunate, a few years ago, to be given the two best Budgerigars at a South African show, by Dr Alf Robertson. One died shortly after being imported but the second, a Grey Green cock of outstanding quality, bred a small number of offspring which still feature in the pedigrees of my present Budgerigars. That South African Grey Green cock proved its quality when it took the best in show award at London & Southern Counties BS area championship. I have an outstanding Skyblue cock in my birdroom at the present time. It was offered to me because its breeder, Joe Nevin of Dublin, Eire, did not have a good enough hen to pair with it. It was bred from one of my cocks so it should blend well with the hens I select as its mates. This sort of co-operation does not occur very often but it is possible when your friends trust you and are prepared to work with you. Another way of obtaining the quality of Budgerigar that you need when you are a champion is to look abroad. With quarantine regulations changing (from January 1, 1994 no quarantine will be required for birds being brought from the European Economic Community into the United Kingdom) it will make it easier to get good stock from continental Europe.

Gren and Pat Norris:

In our experience, the only way to acquire quality stock is to purchase it. On a number of occasions we have exchanged Budgerigars with other fanciers but have yet to be satisfied with the resulting offspring. When one pays a fair price for a Budgerigar there are no obligations on either party. Even so, buying an outcross is never easy, whether it is from a top champion, a less-successful champion or a novice. This is because we are looking for Budgerigars with a background, not simply visual qualities. The best opportunities often come from champions or intermediates who live a long distance away. We are less of a threat to them. Sometimes it is necessary to go abroad for an outcross.

Joe Sabella:

If the opportunity arises I occasionally try to buy an outcross and I also have a network of friends in the hobby with whom I might exchange a bird or two. Exchanging works to the benefit of both parties. I believe I have the necessary size and length in my Budgerigars and their head qualities are good so I try to acquire outcrosses that excel in mask quality. In my experience, spot size regresses, becoming smaller, unless it is continually reinforced.

Do you ever sell the best Blues from your stud?

Derrick Bowley:

What is the point of selling your best birds? The best always stay with me. After all, a good Budgerigar eats only the same amount of seed as a bad one! Though there have been occasions when I have refused a good offer and the bird has died shortly afterwards. I remember a fellow club member who had a wonderful stud of White Border Canaries. He sold the best abroad after claiming that he could soon breed some more. He never did. Never be too eager to let your current-year Blues go. A few years ago I awarded three major specials to Blues and decided that I would like to buy a couple of them. It turned out that I had sold every one of them when they were very young; before they had displayed their full potential. It was suggested that I must have very good Budgerigars if I could afford to sell birds like these. The truth was that I made a mistake. At the time it was within the rules to exhibit Budgerigars under a judge you had bought them from.

Brian Byles:

I never sell my best birds. No one can progress if he or she sells their top birds. Taking that a step further; never sell any Budgerigar unless you are certain it will not be required in your breeding programme. Certainly, never oversell. It is much better to keep too many Budgerigars than not

"Never be too eager to let your current-year Blues go", advises Derrick Bowley. There is no doubt that this young Skyblue cock, which he bred in 1993, will reach maturity in the Bowley birdroom.

enough. At the same time, there is no point in retaining Budgerigars which do not come up the standard that you have set for yourself.

Gren and Pat Norris:

Our very best show birds have never been sold although, on occasions, their high-quality brothers and sisters leave the stud. Equally, a high-quality stock bird is retained in the stud until it is retired from the breeding team. It is almost impossible to acquire top-quality show Budgerigars and if one succumbs to the temptation of money the bird that was sold would be impossible to replace with one of equal quality from elsewhere. In addition, there is much more satisfaction winning with your own birds.

Joe Sabella:

My very best Blues are seldom sold because they provide the wins on the show bench and produce the young that maintain and upgrade the stud. I have sold some very good Blues in the past to breeders who I admire but only after they have produced for me for a couple of breeding seasons. When a bird's progeny is available for breeding there is no great loss in its departure. If no-one was prepared to let good Budgerigars go there would be no progress and many more people would leave the hobby. This is particularly true where beginners and novices are concerned. My pet peeve is the champion who sells only his culls and will not let an aspiring hobbyist have a decent bird.

What, in your opinion, is the degree of difficulty of Blues?

Derrick Bowley:

The most difficult problem I face is of my own making. I find it most difficult to maintain size and, because of my mania for Normals, I am not prepared to use the Opalines which could help. So size is always in my mind when selecting pairings. With selective breeding, maintaining depth of colour poses no problems.

Brian Byles:

Breeding good Skyblues is no more difficult than breeding good Budgerigars of any other colour. Breeding Budgerigars is not difficult. Breeding top quality ones will never be easy.

Gren and Pat Norris:

Looking at Blue Budgerigars as a whole, the two major problems seen on the show bench are lack of size and poor colour. Maintaining size depends upon the strength of a line-bred stud. That is not to say that a well-proportioned, smaller Blue could not be used for breeding, but it would need to be paired with a large mate – as would any progeny. As far as we are concerned, a Blue without strong colour is not worth calling a Blue. Maintaining colour depends very much upon the eye of the breeder. From the moment our Budgerigars begin to feather up we are looking for colour intensity and a brightness that could almost be called iridescence: the sort of colour that the Opalines of old used to possess. Buff feathering is often given as an excuse for loss of colour on many top Budgerigars. In our experience this is only partly true because there is just as much colour variation in

Buffs as there is in those with yellow feathering. When a Blue turns up from our Grey Greens it is very noticeable that it lacks the intensity of colour found in our mainstream Blues, irrespective of its feather type. There are not many out-and-out Buffs in our stud and those that we have are used with care. We never pair a Buff with another Buff but prefer a good, tight-feathered Cinnamon as its mate. Such pairings can produce some very useful stock birds, carrying intermediate feathering, plus the occasional outstanding individual with length, feather and "blow".

Joe Sabella:

I do not find it very difficult to breed Blues of good quality. Recessive varieties are far more difficult. For instance, the problems to be overcome in producing a good Clearwing are enormous. There are some aspects of breeding Blues that can be frustrating. As you improve spot size and mask, the overall feather quality becomes such that you lose colour intensity and the tendency for head flecking increases. Many a good Budgerigar is lost to the show team because of head flecking. This is the sort of challenge that makes our hobby so rewarding.

Are there any tactics that can help you win with Blues?

Derrick Bowley:

A good Budgerigar can be made into a winner by training it and putting it into a nice, clean show cage. When judging I see Budgerigars that have not been properly trained and show cages that have not been cleaned since their last outing. Green feathers in the bottom of cages that contain Blue Budgerigars and new cage labels stuck over old ones indicate an exhibitor who does not deserve to win. I have seen super Budgerigars running around on the show cage floor as though they do not know what the perches are for. A judge has only a limited time and if a Budgerigar does not show itself to its full potential I penalise it. A Budgerigar that is well-trained and put in a clean show cage has a head start. In an ideal world, every judge would place birds in the same order every time but in reality, all judges see Budgerigars differently. Even my son and I do not always agree on which is the best. To cover this, when exhibiting I like to enter two or three Blues in each class and have been quite surprised at the order some judges place them in.

Brian Byles:

Good feeding, good general management and attention to detail. The only factor that determines how many Blues I exhibit at a show is how many are worth showing.

Gren and Pat Norris:

A good specimen will never be a consistent winner unless it has the ability to display its good points to a judge. Some Budgerigars are natural showmen but others require training. All of our Budgerigars are handled regularly when they are in the nest, and onwards, to improve their confidence. When they are weaned they are put in cages, in groups of eight to 12 of similar age. This steadies them and they are placed in show cages for a few minutes, two or three times a week. As soon as they show signs of moulting they are moved to an indoor flight to enable them to develop fully. Those that display show potential are brought back, in groups of eight to 10, into 6ft long flight cages as they end their moult, with the sexes kept separated. From this point training intensifies. They are sprayed heavily several times a week and placed in show cages to dry out. This increases steadiness, improves and retains condition. Any bird needing extra training is put with an older, steadier bird to learn the ropes. Just prior to showing spraying takes place daily (and we mean soaking) and this continues up to the day before the show. Plucking of the mask takes place on the day before the show. On the morning of the show, birds are checked again and any showing blood or dirt are hand-washed. Tails are straightened in hot water and dried on tissue paper. Any bird that is not fit or feather-perfect is removed from the show team. Our show cages are always clean and their perches are always firm. Plenty of seed is placed in the cages and soaked groats are offered in finger drawers after judging has taken place. The birds are placed in the cages and the labels fixed. Cloth covers are placed over the cages to reduce disturbance. On arrival at the show hall, each bird is rechecked and any that is not in perfect condition is returned to the car. We generally enter three Blues in the cock classes but hen entries tend to be singles. By entering three we can show birds that excel in different features and have a greater chance of benching one which catches a particular judge's eye. We know which one we prefer, but the judge sometimes sees things differently.

Joe Sabella:

It is not only necessary to have a Budgerigar of good quality. The bird has to possess other important qualities if it is to win. First of all, condition is important. Several weeks before the show, all potential show birds should be examined one by one. All broken or frayed feathers should be gently removed. Proper spraying is important as is show cage training. Presenting the bird in a clean, shining show cage is essential. That is all the breeder can do. The rest is up to the bird; whether it shows properly when in front of the judge. If you are fortunate, the judge will favour your type of Budgerigar.

Gren and Pat Norris generally enter three Blues in the cock classes to increase the chances of catching a judge's eye. This Skyblue cock, bred by the partners, would take some beating no matter who the judge is.

How do you go about judging Blues?

Derrick Bowley:

Any fault can prevent a Budgerigar from winning. However, as I have never seen a perfect Budgerigar, I can only assess each bird and make appropriate allowances for its faults. My procedure begins with checking whether every exhibit fits the description (colour, variety, sex and age) of the class, in the schedule. I then look for a possible winner, place it at the front, and compare the rest with it. Sometimes the bird I chose first stays at the front but, at other times, it moves down as other exhibits show themselves to be superior. When it comes to judging, there are no special features that make Normal Blues any different from Normal Greens, Greys and Grey Greens. Over many, many years I have exhibited my Blues under numerous judges and have adjudicated alongside others at literally hundreds of shows. Never in that time have I encountered a dishonest judge. There are, of course, honest differences of opinion but these are to be expected. By and large, this is a very honest hobby and I am proud to be associated with it. I have no disagreement with the scale of points and colour standards for Blues. Some fanciers say that the "Ideal" has been surpassed, but I do not agree. There ARE Budgerigars that exceed 10in (25.4cm) in length but most of this can be accounted for by an overlong tail – which spoils the bird's balance. If you cut out the picture of a the Ideal Budgerigar, painted so well by Eric Peake, or the Ideal model and place either in a show cage you will see what I mean. I have yet to see a live Budgerigar to equal it.

Brian Byles:

Judging Skyblues is little different from judging other varieties. If I am given a large class, such as when I judged the Blue classes at The BS Club Show in 1991, I discard the "also-rans" first. There are usually one or two exhibits that are better than the rest. These are placed at the top, to the left of the judging trestle. Then each of the remaining birds is compared with them and moved until they are in order. I like large Budgerigars with feathering that is not too coarse – intermediate Buffs – carrying wide shoulders and matching heads. I like to see large, round spots on a deep mask. Unfortunately, too many Normal Skyblues carry opaline markings on their wings and necks. Although I dislike having to place a flecked-headed bird first in its class, if it is vastly superior to the rest of the exhibits I will do so. The problem is that this can lead to there being a predominance of flecked and ticked birds in the line-up for the major specials and then there is little chance of picking a clean-headed bird for the top prize. Unless flecked Budgerigars are banned entirely there is always a chance that they will get among the specials. But why should flecked-headed Budgerigars be banned? Most Budgerigars have other faults which are just as serious and there is no talk of banning these. Exhibiting under any judge is a lottery – unless you really understand their likes and dislikes. Specialist judges are certainly necessary for varieties such as Recessive Pieds, Clearwings and Lutinos but most judges, if they are worth their salt, should be able to judge Blues. I do feel that having good Budgerigars is a prerequisite of being able to judge good Budgerigars but not all good breeders are good judges and not all top exhibitors are good judges. In the same vein, not all good judges are good breeders of Budgerigars. Many good breeders, even when they know what is required, lack the concentration necessary for the duration of judging to make a good job of placing the awards.

Gren and Pat Norris:

Judging Blues must, of course, always be in accordance with the Budgerigar Society's scale of points. First, we take a brief look at every exhibit in a class and, with a big class, this permits us to discount a number of birds that obviously have no chance. A "marker" bird is chosen (one which, at first sight could be the winner) and, thereafter, judging consists of making visual comparisons between that and the rest. This arrives at a line of birds placed in an initial order. We than make a closer examination, taking into account showmanship and the finer points of the variety. We hate to see Blues with patchy or insipid colour, dropped tails, poor stance and lack of head quality. The winning bird will be the one that displays least faults on the day – all things being equal. For a winning Blue to go further it must sparkle with good health, strong colour and showmanship. When it comes to showing our own Budgerigars, we have no qualms about exhibiting them under judges who are not Blue specialists. It is more important to learn what a particular judge's foibles are so that you can bench a Budgerigar that appeals to him or her. The BS scale of points for Blues is very fair, though perhaps a little more recognition of colour would be an improvement. It would also be helpful if the BS issued colour swatches clearly defining desired shades.

Joe Sabella:

The approach to judging a class of Blue Budgerigars depends on how many exhibits there are in the class. If it is a large class (20 – 40) I carefully look at each Budgerigar and try to persuade the ones on the cage floors to perch. After that first assessment, I remove from competition those that stand no chance of a placing. That usually cuts the field in half. As I go along I note the better specimens and these are moved to the left of the judging trestle. If there are one or two outstanding exhibits the job is made easier. If the exhibits are finely balanced I have to start examining their finer points such as: head flecking, broken or missing flights, whether it is standing clear of the perch. A systematic elimination process leaves me with the best specimens. I believe a judge must be decisive and confident when making his decisions. A questionable exhibit should be left in contention until its true merit has been established.

How do you see the future of Blues?

Derrick Bowley:

Blue Budgerigars have an important part to play in the future advancement of the hobby. An increasing number of Blue Budgerigars are taking top awards at major shows and, more important, they are in the hands of several very experienced breeders who know how to maintain and improve them. Compare the entries in the Blue classes with 25 years ago. There has been a 100 per cent increase. From the large number of enquiries I receive, asking for advice on Blue Budgerigars, it is obvious that there is much enthusiasm for the colour and if this trend continues we could see

Normal Blues overtaking Normal Greens. It very nearly happened at the 1991 BS Club Show when 369 Light Greens and 345 Normal Blues were entered. Blues will more than hold their own in the years to come.

Brian Byles:

Having seen some outstanding Skyblues in the past couple of years, I am sure that there is a very bright future for the variety.

Gren and Pat Norris:

In our opinion, Blue Budgerigars will continue to be at the forefront on the show bench. Blues have been around for an awfully long time and in all that time they have always taken their share of major awards. The mail we receive proves that the beautiful colours displayed by Blues are an attraction the world over. This popularity will ensure that any new mutations that appear in the future will be immediately paired with Blues and this, in itself, will protect the variety. History has shown that various Budgerigar varieties have had peaks of popularity, but Normals and Blues have stayed the course and will continue to do so. Blue Budgerigars will continue to make progress and we believe that the Blues of the future will be larger in all departments with more lateral feathering on the head, increased feather blow above the eye and greater depth of mask. We have every intention that our own Blue Budgerigars will be a part of this development.

Joe Sabella:

In years past, Greens and Grey Greens won the top awards at most shows. In the USA Light Greens are the strongest variety with Grey Greens in second place. However, in the past couple of years I have detected that Blues are coming to the forefront. When I visited Jo Mannes, the best Budgerigars I saw were Blues. Many of the top winners at the Budgerigar Society Club Show and at Budgerigar World Show have been Blues. The Budgerigar that won two years running at the top show in Brazil was a Blue. I believe that Blues will come more and more into prominence in the 1990s.

CHAPTER 7

COLOUR EXPECTATIONS

The subject of Budgerigar colour expectations could fill a book on its own - in fact it HAS filled a book and anyone who wants to delve deeper into the subject should read Taylor and Warner's *Genetics for Budgerigar Breeders.*

Understanding genetics CAN help when it comes to breeding good Budgerigars - particularly when recessive varieties are involved - but it must be stressed that many of the breeders who have bred the best Budgerigars in the world have had only a sketchy knowledge of the subject. So, if you find the subject difficult to understand you will be in good company, and should not worry unduly. For the benefit of those who are interested, and to assist understanding of some of the pairings recommended by the experts, there follow a few examples of how colour expectations can be calculated.

The first fact that needs to be understood is that, in every case, there are TWO factors controlling every individual colour and variety. In this book, the letters used to denote these are not necessarily the ones that are used in serious text books, but have been chosen to make it easier for the inexperienced to understand. So Blue is represented by the letter "B" and Green by "G". When it comes to looking at Dark factor Budgerigars, "L" will represent a light factor and "D" will stand for a dark factor. Each colour series comes in three levels of darkness; Light, Medium and Dark. In the Blue series these equate with Skyblue, Cobalt and Mauve while in the Green series they equal Light Green, Dark Green and Olive. Like colour, darkness is controlled by TWO factors. To make it simple, let us say a Light has two light factors ("LL"), a Dark has two dark factors ("DD") and a Medium has one light factor and one dark ("LD"). When two Budgerigars mate, each gives ONE of its colour factors to each chick. The possible combinations can be represented by a grid of four squares.

So what happens when two Medium Budgerigars mate and each parent passes on one of its factors to each chick?

		Medium	
		L	D
Medium	L	LL	LD
	D	LD	DD

A quarter of the chicks will be "LL" (Light), a half will be "LD" (Medium) and a quarter will be "DD" (Dark). Translated into colours, this means that two Cobalts paired together will produce Skyblues, Cobalts and Mauves.

Now let us look at the relationship between a dominant (Green) and a recessive (Blue). A Green Budgerigar's two colour letters are both "G"s. So a Green is "GG". In the same way "BB" indicates a Blue. The next grid shows what happens when a Green mates with a Blue.

		Green	
		G	G
Blue	B	GB	GB
	B	GB	GB

All of the combinations – hence all of the chicks – are the same, "GB" which describes a Budgerigar that looks like a Green but can produce Blues. It is called a Green split Blue (usually written Green/Blue). Let us take it one step further and see what happens when two Green split Blues are mated together.

		Green split Blue	
		G	B
Green split Blue	G	GG	GB
	B	GB	BB

A quarter of the chicks will be "GG" (Greens), a half will be "GB" (Green split Blue, like their parents) and a quarter will be "BB" – Blues! That is how Blue Budgerigars can be bred from two that look just like Greens. If you make your own grid to check what happens when you pair two Blues together (BB x BB), you will not be surprised to find that they will produce all Blues.

By combining the results of the grids it is possible to include combinations of Skyblue, Cobalt, Mauve, Light Green, Dark Green and Olive into your calculations. However, there is a complication when you come to Dark Green/Blue in that the colours they produce are influenced by whether the Dark factor has been inherited with the Green component of the bird or the Blue. Typically, a Dark Greens/Blue Type I has its Dark factor connected with Green and, as a consequence, tends to produce more Dark Greens/Blue and Skyblues when paired with a Skyblue. A Dark Green/Blue Type II has its dark factor connected with Blue and, when paired with a Skyblue, tends to produce more Light Greens/Blue and Cobalts.

The above description of the dominance of Greens over Blues can be carried straight over to explain the relationship between Greys and Blues but, in this case, it is the Grey which is dominant and not the Green. Indeed, the Grey factor is dominant to Green as well and produces Grey Greens. To be strictly accurate, a Grey is a Blue with a Grey factor added and a Grey Green is a Green with a Grey factor added, but to simplify the following calculation it will be considered as a factor in its own right and allocated the letter "R". So a double-factor Grey (DF) will be designated "RR" and a single-factor Grey (SF) will be represented by "RB" (one Grey factor and one Blue factor).

The following grid demonstrates what happens when a Grey (DF) is paired with a Blue:

		Grey (DF)	
		R	R
Blue	B	RB	RB
	B	RB	RB

All the chicks will be "RB" (single-factor Greys), looking like Greys but capable of producing Blues if paired appropriately.

When dealing with Blues, there is another mutation that must be taken into account; the Violet. As far as colour expectations are concerned it is best to treat Violet as a simple dominant, just as Green is dominant to Blue. However, what complicates matters is that the wonderful violet coloration can only be seen in its full glory when Violet factor is combined with Blue and Medium. A visual Violet is, in fact, a Violet Cobalt. When combined with the other colours (Skyblue, Mauve, Light Green, Dark Green, Olive, Grey and Grey Green), the Violet factor has a darkening and richening effect. This results in Violet Light Greens being mistaken for Dark Greens, Violet Skyblues being called "Cobalts" and Violet Dark Greens being entered in classes for Olives. If it is Violets, rather than Greys, that interest you the one can be substituted for the other in the last grid.

Many newcomers to the Fancy are surprised when a Blue appears in the nest of two Greys. Following the example of the grid which showed two Greens/Blue being paired together to show what happens when two single-factor Greys are paired together. They will produce double-factor Greys, single-factor Greys and Blues. Try it! Now see what happens if you pair a single-factor Grey Green/Blue with a Blue. You will find that when Grey, Green and Blue are all in the genetic make-up of a single Budgerigar it is capable of producing Grey Greens, Greys, Blues and Greens.

For those who have no wish to calculate colour expectations, the following tables will prove useful.

TABLE 1: Pairings involving Skyblues, Cobalts and Mauves.
(with theoretical percentage expectations)

Pairing*	Expectations (cocks and hens)
Skyblue × Skyblue	100% Skyblue
Skyblue × Cobalt	50% Skyblue 50% Cobalt
Skyblue × Mauve	100% Cobalt
Cobalt × Cobalt	25% Skyblue 50% Cobalt 25% Mauve
Cobalt × Mauve	50% Cobalt 50% Mauve
Mauve × Mauve	100% Mauve

* *(It makes no difference which colour is the cock and which is the hen)*

TABLE 2: Pairings involving Greens and Blues
(with theoretical percentage expectations)

Pairing*	Expectations (cocks and hens)
Green × Green	100% Green
Green × Blue	100% Green/Blue
Green × Green/Blue	50% Green 50% Green/Blue
Green/Blue × Green/Blue	25% Green 50% Green/Blue 25% Blue
Green/Blue × Blue	50% Green/Blue 50% Blue
Blue × Blue	100% Blue

* *(It makes no difference which colour is the cock and which is the hen)*

TABLE 3: Pairings involving Greys and Blues
(with theoretical percentage expectations)

Pairing*	Expectations (cocks and hens)
Blue × Blue	100% Blue
Blue × Grey (DF)	100% Grey (SF)
Blue × Grey (SF)	50% Grey (SF) 50% Blue
Grey (SF) × Grey (SF)	25% Grey (DF) 50% Grey (SF) 25% Blue
Grey (SF) × Grey (DF)	50% Grey (DF) 50% Grey (SF)
Grey (DF) × Grey (DF)	100% Grey (DF)

* *(It makes no difference which colour is the cock and which is the hen)*

Further copies of this book and details about others in the "All about ..." series can be obtained from:

F. Wright,
31 Redford Avenue,
Wallington,
Surrey, SM6 9DT.

Telephone or
Fax: 081-647 6378

Ask for details of quantity and club discounts